P9-CCB-815

Student Edition

Bring Science Alive!
Exploring Science Practices

*NGSS is a registered trademark of Achieve. Neither Achieve nor the lead states and partners that developed the Next Generation Science Standards was involved in the production of, and does not endorse, this product.

Chief Executive Officer
Bert Bower

Chief Operating Officer
Amy Larson

Director of Product Development
Maria Favata

Strategic Product Manager
Nathan Wellborne

Senior Science Content Developer
Ariel Stein

Curriculum Consultants
Kim Merlino
Joan Westley

Program Editors
David Fraker
Mikaila Garfinkel
Edward Helderop
Rebecca Ou
Ginger Wu

Editorial Consultant
Glenda Stewart

Production Manager
Jodi Forrest

Operations & Software Manager
Marsha Ifurung

Designer
Sarah Osentowski

Art Direction
Julia Foug

Teachers' Curriculum Institute
PO Box 1327
Rancho Cordova, CA 95741

Customer Service: 800-497-6138
www.teachtci.com

Copyright © 2015 by Teachers' Curriculum Institute.
No parts of the publication may be reproduced without written permission from the publisher.
Printed in the United States of America.

ISBN 978-1-58371-968-8
2 3 4 5 6 7 8 9 10 -WC- 20 19 18 17 16 15

Manufactured by Webcrafters, Inc., Madison, WI
United States of America, May 2015, Job # 121650

SUSTAINABLE FORESTRY INITIATIVE

Certified Sourcing

www.sfiprogram.org

SFI-00617

Science Advisory Board

Marilyn Chambliss, Ph.D.
Associate Professor of Reading Education,
Emerita at the University of Maryland
University of Maryland, College Park

Angelo Collins, Ph.D.
Associate Dean
School of Education and Counseling Psychology
Santa Clara University
Santa Clara, CA

Ron Korenich, Ed.D.
Educational Consultant
Retired Coordinator of Elementary Education
for the Fox Chapel Area School District
Pittsburgh, Pennsylvania

Kathleen Peasley, Ph.D.
Assistant Superintendent for Academic Services
Grand Ledge Public Schools
Michigan

Steve Schneider, Ph.D.
Senior Program Director of Science, Technology,
Engineering, and Mathematics
WestEd

Jerome M. Shaw, Ph.D.
Associate Professor of Science Education
University of California, Santa Cruz

Andrew Shouse, Ph.D.
Associate Director of the Institute for Science
and Math Education and Assistant Research
Professor of Learning Sciences
University of Washington

Nancy Butler Songer, Ph.D.
Professor of Science Education and Learning
Technologies and Director of the Center for
Essential Science
University of Michigan

Donald B. Young, Ph.D.
Dean of the College of Education
and Professor of Science Education
University of Hawaii at Manoa

Science Content Scholars

Matthew Bobrowsky, Ph.D.
University of Maryland

John Czworkowski, Ph.D.
University of California, San Diego

Tanya Dewey, Ph.D.
University of Michigan

Andrew P. Norton, Ph.D.
*University of California,
Santa Cruz*

About the Next Generation Science Standards

The Next Generation Science Standards (NGSS) describe the science skills and knowledge all students need to know to succeed in college, careers, and citizenship. The standards were developed by a panel that collaborated with representatives from 26 lead states. They are based on *A Framework for K–12 Science Education*, which was written by a team of scientists, engineers, and science educators, and published by the National Research Council in 2012.

The NGSS were released in Spring 2013, and TCI's science instructional program, *Bring Science Alive!*, was developed to meet them.

One part of the disciplinary core idea PS4.B: Electromagnetic Radiation focuses on how much light is able to pass through different materials, including materials that completely block out light and create a shadow on surfaces beyond them.

Each performance expectation has three dimensions: disciplinary core ideas, scientific and engineering practices, and crosscutting concepts. Together, these describe what students should understand and be able to accomplish at each grade level.

What are performance expectations, and how does *Bring Science Alive!* prepare students to demonstrate mastery?

Performance expectations describe what all students should be able to do at the completion of a unit of study. They guide assessment and are supported by the details in the disciplinary core ideas, practices, and crosscutting concepts. Many performance expectations are followed by clarification statements and assessment boundaries. Clarification statements provide examples and details, and assessment boundaries limit what students should be tested on.

Bring Science Alive! prepares students to meet the performance expectations. Performance expectations are identified in the Student Text at the beginning of each unit and each lesson. They are also incorporated into the investigations in the online Presentations for students to practice.

How are the Next Generation Science Standards related to Common Core standards?

The NGSS are aligned to the Common Core State Standards for English Language Arts & Literacy in History/Social Studies, Science, and Technical Subjects and Common Core State Standards for Mathematics.

Similarly, *Bring Science Alive!* is aligned to Common Core English and Mathematics. For example, all Reading Furthers in the Student Text align with the Reading Standards for Informational Text K–5. Interactive Tutorials address Common Core reading and writing standards. Lesson content and investigations are aligned with Common Core Mathematics, such as when students learn about measurement units and tools and graphing.

What are Disciplinary Core Ideas, and how does *Bring Science Alive!* meet them?

Disciplinary core ideas focus instruction on the foundational knowledge students need for success in each grade. Core ideas build from year to year, from Kindergarten to Grade 12, in learning progressions that revisit each topic several times, each time with greater depth and sophistication. Therefore, students are expected to understand the core ideas that were taught in previous grades.

For these reasons, teachers and parents may find fewer topics taught in each grade than they have seen previously. Additionally, many topics are taught in different grades than they were under previous standards. By limiting the content at each grade, students are able to learn with deeper understanding.

Bring Science Alive! guides students through these core ideas as they read their Student Text, complete Interactive Tutorials, carry out hands-on and online investigations, and write, draw, diagram, and calculate in their Interactive Student Notebooks.

Performance expectation K-PS3-2. has students design and build a structure that minimizes the effect of sunlight on a certain area.

What are Science and Engineering Practices, and how does *Bring Science Alive!* meet them?

Science and engineering practices describe the abilities students should develop to engage in science and engineering. Students use these eight practices to master the principles described in the core ideas. The practices also help students understand how professional scientists and engineers answer questions and solve problems.

- **?** Asking questions and defining problems
- Developing and using models
- Planning and carrying out investigations
- Analyzing and interpreting data
- Using mathematics and computational thinking
- Constructing explanations and designing solutions
- Engaging in argument from evidence
- Obtaining, evaluating, and communicating information

Every lesson in *Bring Science Alive!* develops science and engineering practices in the online lesson Presentation. Practices are used explicitly and help teach the lesson's core ideas. Each of the eight practices is taught at every grade level with increasing sophistication from grade to grade.

The science and engineering practices Analyzing and Interpreting Data have students analyze data collected from tests in order to decide if an object is working as it is intended to.

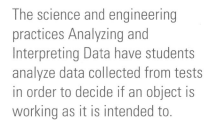

What are Crosscutting Concepts, and how does *Bring Science Alive!* meet them?

The crosscutting concepts are used to organize students' understanding of science and engineering in the same way that scientists and engineers do. They give students specific ideas to consider when learning about a new topic. These ideas are intended to help students understand the topics at a deeper level.

In addition to supporting core ideas, the seven crosscutting concepts support one another. They are listed below with descriptions of their importance for all upper elementary students.

Patterns Students observe patterns and use these observations to describe phenomena and as evidence.

Cause and Effect Students identify causes that make observable patterns and design simple tests to support or refute their ideas about causes.

Scale, Proportion, and Quantity Students make relative comparisons of objects (e.g. bigger and smaller; hotter and colder; faster and slower), and measure length in standard units.

Systems and System Models Students learn to describe objects and organisms using the objects' parts and recognize that systems have parts that work together.

Energy and Matter Students recognize that objects can be broken into smaller pieces, assembled into larger pieces, or change shape.

Structure and Function Students relate the shape and stability of structures and objects to their functions.

Stability and Change Students observe that some things stay the same, while other change slowly or rapidly.

Each lesson is carefully developed to explain and integrate the crosscutting concept with core ideas.

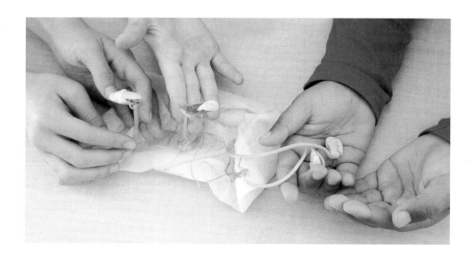

While learning about the crosscutting concept Structure and Function, students will learn about the relationship between the stability and shape of natural and designed object's structures and the structures' functions.

Connections to Engineering, Technology, and Applications of Science

The Next Generation Science Standards address engineering design as a process similar to, and just as important as, scientific inquiry. Engineering design is divided into three broad steps, each of which encompasses several of the science and engineering practices.

The steps are described by the grades K–2 engineering design performance expectations, listed below.

- *K-2-ETS1-1. Ask questions, make observations, and gather information about a situation people want to change to define a simple problem that can be solved through the development of a new or improved object or tool.*

- *K-2-ETS1-2. Develop a simple sketch, drawing, or physical model to illustrate how the shape of an object helps it function as needed to solve a given problem.*

- *K-2-ETS1-3. Analyze data from tests of two objects designed to solve the same problem to compare the strengths and weaknesses of how each performs.*

Bring Science Alive! provides many opportunities for students to understand the work of engineers and use the engineering design process to solve problems relevant to the scientific knowledge they are simultaneously developing.

Engineering, Technology, and Applications of Science in the Investigations

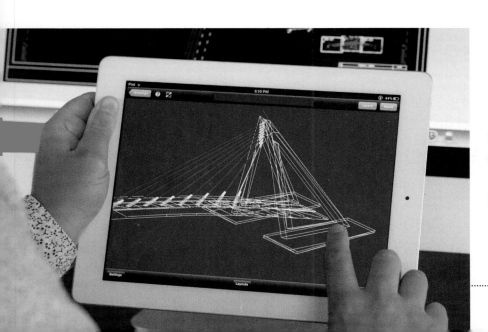

When students study the uses of different materials in Unit 2, they learn how engineers design a bridge to help people cross a river.

Engineering, Technology, and Applications of Science in the Student Text

Interactions of Science, Technology, Society and the Environment in the Student Text

While learning in Unit 2 how small objects can be assembled in many ways, students read how people can make tree houses by reusing parts of other structures.

Connections to the Nature of Science

The science and engineering practices describe how to engage in scientific inquiry. The disciplinary core ideas describe existing scientific knowledge. The crosscutting concepts provide a framework for connecting scientific knowledge. Students integrate these dimensions of learning when they learn what kinds of knowledge are scientific, how scientists develop that knowledge, and about the wide spectrum of people who engage in science.

Nature of Science in the Student Text

Nature of Science in the Investigations

One of the basic understandings about the nature of science described in NGSS is that investigations use different tools and procedures to study the world.

How to Use This Program

1 The teacher begins each lesson with a **Presentation** that facilitates the lesson and the investigation.

2 In the Presentations, students participate in a hands-on **investigation** that blends the core ideas, science practices, and crosscutting concepts of NGSS.

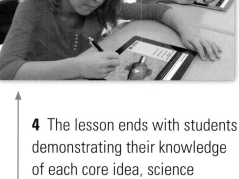

3a In the online **Student Subscription**, students expand their knowledge through reading the Student Text, completing an Interactive Tutorial, and processing what they've learned in the **Interactive Student Notebook**.

3b Alternatively, students can read from the **Student Edition** and complete a consumable Interactive Student Notebook.

4 The lesson ends with students demonstrating their knowledge of each core idea, science practice, and crosscutting concept through a variety of paper and online **assessments**.

Literacy in Science

The Next Generation Science Standards were developed to work in tandem with the Common Core State Standards to ensure that students develop literacy skills through learning science. *Bring Science Alive!* builds on this synergy by emphasizing reading, writing, speaking and listening, and language skills while guiding students in developing their science knowledge.

Key Points from the ELA Common Core	*Bring Science Alive!*

Reading

Informational and literary texts are balanced with at least 50% of reading time devoted to expository texts.	CCSS changes the emphasis in reading from being based primarily on literary texts to being balanced between literary and informational texts. *Bring Science Alive!* reflects this balance in its text. Each lesson has several sections of purely informational text that explains the content of that lesson. Each lesson is followed by a Reading Further, which blends literary and informational style text to engage students with the content even further.
Establishes a "staircase" of increasing complexity in what students must be able to read as they move throughout the grades.	*Bring Science Alive!* is written with close attention paid to the text complexity to make sure it fits into the "staircase" of increasingly sophisticated text that students should read as they progress through the grades. However, within each grade's text, there is variation in the complexity to ensure that there is challenging text for all students.
Emphasizes the close reading of text to determine main ideas, supporting details, and evidence.	The digital Interactive Tutorials encourage close reading of the text. They require students to answer questions using evidence from the text. Answering the questions requires a clear understanding of the main ideas and other details provided in the section.

Writing

Three types of writing are emphasized from the earliest grades—writing to persuade, writing to inform/explain, and writing to convey experience.	NGSS and *Bring Science Alive!* require students to use all three types of writing emphasized by CCSS. In the investigations, students are often asked to construct written arguments to persuade their classmates of their explanation of a scientific concept. They also write accounts of their experiences in these activities and investigations, describing details of the experiment or design process. In the Interactive Student Notebook, students write explanations to demonstrate their understanding of the scientific concepts described in the text.
Effective use of evidence is central throughout the writing standards.	In all three types of writing, students are expected to use evidence appropriately to support their claims. They are given support in identifying key details which will serve most effectively as evidence. They also reflect on their use of evidence in various contexts to build an explicit understanding of the role evidence plays in science and argument in general.
Routine production of writing appropriate for a range of tasks, purposes, and audiences is emphasized.	Students routinely write in all of *Bring Science Alive!*'s curricula. The program emphasizes the flexibility and usefulness of writing to accomplish a variety of assignments. It also gives students exposure to the different expectations in writing for different purposes and audiences.

Key Points from the ELA Common Core	*Bring Science Alive!*
Speaking and Listening	
Participation in rich, structured academic conversations in one-on-one, small-group, and whole class situations is emphasized in the standards.	Classrooms using *Bring Science Alive!* will regularly have structured science talks in which students reflect on their experiences and understanding of the investigations. They will also have regular discussions in smaller groups, ranging from discussions with a partner to groups of four or five students. These discussions are designed to build clear communication skills that are critical to success in science and all other fields of study.
Contributing accurate, relevant information; responding to and building on what others have said; and making comparisons and contrasts are important skills for productive conversations.	In all discussions, students are given support to help them learn to contribute relevant and accurate details and evidence. The cooperative tolerant classroom conventions emphasized throughout all of TCI's curricula encourage students to respond to and build on ideas and arguments presented by other students. *Bring Science Alive!* uses NGSS's crosscutting concepts to help students to compare and contrast relevant experiences across domains of science in discussions.

Language	
Demonstrate command of the conventions of English when writing and speaking.	Throughout all the components of *Bring Science Alive!*, students are expected to demonstrate command of the conventions of written and spoken English.
Acquire and use general academic and domain-specific words.	*Bring Science Alive!* has a progression of increasingly sophisticated vocabulary built into it with complexity suggested by the language used in NGSS. It is designed to emphasize key words used throughout a lesson or unit of study without overwhelming students with too many unfamiliar words. Every component of *Bring Science Alive!* makes use of the vocabulary and includes activities to help solidify comprehension.
Focus on developing skills to determine or clarify the meaning of unknown words or phrases.	Other science-related words which may be unfamiliar to students, but do not play a key role in the overall understanding of a concept, are defined in context. This gives students ample opportunity and support in determining and clarifying the meaning of unfamiliar words using clues from the text.

Considerate Text

Sample Graphic Organizer

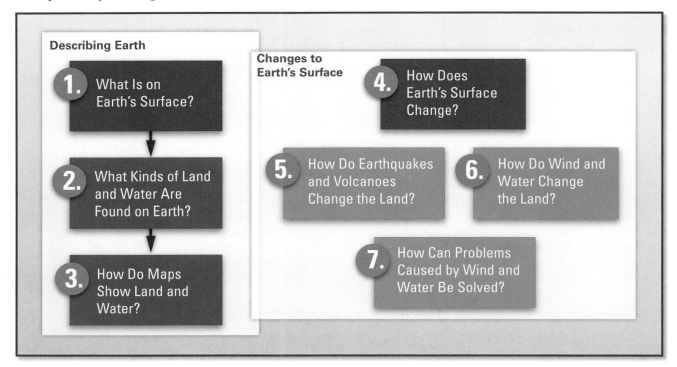

You are about to discover that *Bring Science Alive!* is both interesting and easy to understand. That's because our authors wrote it as a "considerate text," which is another way of saying that it makes readers want to read it. Here are some ways this book is considerate for all levels of readers:

- Each unit is carefully mapped out so that one lesson builds on the next. So, you will find a clear graphic organizer, like the one above, in each unit opener. The graphic organizer shows how all the lessons in the unit relate to one another. A **purple** lesson is the main idea, **blue** stands for lessons that support the main idea, and **green** and **red** lessons take those ideas even further.

- Short lessons make it easier for you to understand and remember what each one is about.

- Information is presented in easy-to-manage chunks for better understanding.

- Important new words are in bold type. These words are defined in the glossary in the back of the book.

- Photos, illustrations, and diagrams provide additional information about the topic on the page.

How To Read the Table of Contents

The **lesson title** is also the lesson's Essential Question.

Each lesson has a **crosscutting concept** or 'theme' associated with it.

The **unit name** tells you the overall topic of the unit.

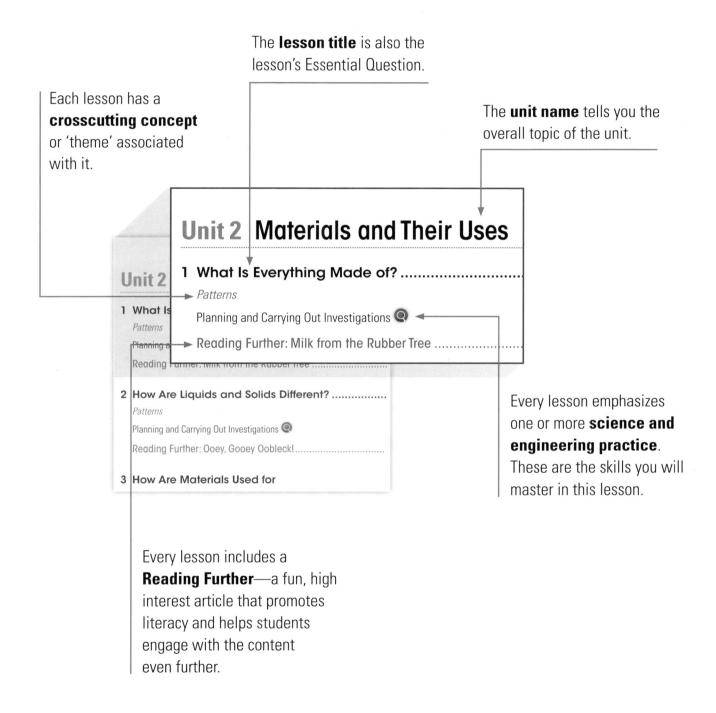

Every lesson emphasizes one or more **science and engineering practice**. These are the skills you will master in this lesson.

Every lesson includes a **Reading Further**—a fun, high interest article that promotes literacy and helps students engage with the content even further.

Contents

Unit 1 Plant and Animal Survival

Unit 2 Materials and Their Uses

Unit 3 Earth's Surface

Plant and Animal Survival

You walk in the desert looking for signs of life. You come across a plant poking out of the sand. A beautiful caterpillar is crawling on a leaf. You look closer. The caterpillar is chewing on the leaf tip. How do plants and animals survive in the places they live?

Unit Contents

Unit 1 Overview

Graphic Organizer: This unit is structured to establish the fundamental relationship between the **diversity of life** in a given habitat and the **needs of plants and animals** living there.

1. What Kinds of Living Things Are There?

2. What Do Plants and Animals Need to Survive?

3. How Do Plants and Animals Depend on Each Other?

4. Why Do Plants and Animals Live in Some Places and Not in Others?

5. How Do Plants and Animals Survive in a Rainforest?

6. How Do Plants and Animals Survive in a Desert?

7. How Do Plants and Animals Survive in a Pond?

8. How Do Plants and Animals Survive in the Ocean?

NGSS Next Generation Science Standards

Performance Expectations

2-LS2-1. Plan and conduct an investigation to determine if plants need sunlight and water to grow.

2-LS2-2. Develop a simple model that mimics the function of an animal in dispersing seeds or pollinating plants.

2-LS4-1. Make observations of plants and animals to compare the diversity of life in different habitats.

Disciplinary Core Ideas

LS2.A: Interdependent Relationships in Ecosystems

• Plants depend on water and light to grow.

• Plants depend on animals for pollination or to move their seeds around.

LS4.D: Biodiversity and Humans

• There are many different kinds of living things in any area, and they exist in different places on land and in water.

ETS1.B: Developing Possible Solutions

• Designs can be conveyed through sketches, drawings, or physical models. These representations are useful in communicating ideas for a problem's solutions to other people.

Crosscutting Concepts

Cause and Effect

• Events have causes that generate observable patterns.

Structure and Function

• The shape and stability of structures of natural and designed objects are related to their function(s).

 **Developing and Using Models**

 **Planning and Carrying Out Investigations**

I Wonder...

What do animals need to survive?

How do plants and animals survive in a pond?

What lives in the ocean?

What Kinds of Living Things Are There?

Science Words

living thing

Look around you, and you will find living things. How are they alike and different?

1. Living Things

Visit a park, and you will see many things. Squirrels may be climbing trees. Ducks may be swimming in a pond. Children may be riding bikes. How are these things alike and different?

 NGSS **2-LS4-1.** Make observations of plants and animals to compare the diversity of life in different habitats.

LS4.D. There are many different kinds of living things in any area, and they exist in different places on land and in water.

 **Planning and Carrying Out Investigations**

Ducks, squirrels, ferns, and trees
are all **living things**. Living things
live and grow. They make more living
things like themselves. Living things
include tiny ants and huge trees. You
are a living thing, too. All plants and
animals are living things.

Rocks, bikes, and water are not
living things. Nonliving things do not
grow. They cannot make more things
like themselves.

Anywhere you live, you can find
living things around you. You can find
them on land or in water. What kinds
of living things have you seen today?

The squirrel and the
tree are living things.

2. Kinds of Animals

Think of all the kinds of animals you know about. How many different kinds of animals can you name?

There are millions of kinds of animals on Earth! Animals can be found in almost all places on Earth, in water and on land. Fish live in water. Squirrels live on land. Ducks swim in water, but they lay their eggs on land.

Animals come in many different shapes, colors, and sizes.

Each kind of animal is different. A honeybee has six legs and two wings. Its round, furry body is yellow with black stripes. A giraffe is tall with a long neck and four thin legs. It has brown patches on its body. Color, shape, and size are ways to describe a kind of animal.

Plants stay in one place, but most animals can move about. Owls can fly. Sharks swim. Rabbits hop. Cheetahs run very fast. Worms slither underground. One way to tell one kind of animal from another is by looking at how it moves.

This owl is a kind of animal that has wings to fly.

3. Kinds of Plants

Rose bushes and apple trees are kinds of plants. What other different kinds of plants can you name?

There are thousands of different kinds of plants on Earth. Plants can be found in many different places on Earth, on land and in water.

Plants come in many different shapes, sizes, and colors.

Plants come in many shapes, sizes, and colors. Some plants are taller than buildings. Others are so small that they are hard to see. Many plants have green leaves, but the shapes of the leaves are different. Plant flowers and fruits can be many different colors. Some plants are vines that crawl up buildings or trees.

Plants make more plants in different ways. Some have fruits with seeds inside. Some have cones. Plant seeds move to new places in different ways. Some fall to the ground. Some blow away in the wind. Other plants do not make seeds at all.

This pinecone holds many seeds.

4. Observing Nature

Ecologists are scientists who study living things in an area. They may sit and watch for many hours. They try not to disturb the living things.

How do they know what kinds of animals or plants they see? They look carefully. An insect and a spider are about the same size, but an insect has six legs and a spider has eight legs. An oak and an elm are both trees. But the shapes of their leaves are not the same.

Scientists look for patterns when making observations.

These scientists take notes about each plant or animal. They may draw or take pictures. A picture of a plant's leaves could show their shape and color. Notes about a bird might include the colors of its wings, eyes, or tail.

Ecologists look for patterns. They may find some kinds of insects only under fallen branches. A kind of butterfly may feed on only one kind of plant. A kind of bird may nest in only one kind of tree. Ecologists learn a lot by observing living things.

You can tell a spider from an insect by the number of legs it has.

Lesson Summary
Many kinds of living things can be found in any area, on land or in water. Ecologists look for patterns in the living things they find in an area.

Amazon Adventure

Climb aboard a boat tour down the Amazon River. What kinds of plants and animals will you see?

Take a seat, folks, and get ready for the adventure of your life! You are going to see some plants and animals that you have never seen.

As we float down the river, be sure to look around you. Look in the water and on the land. Living things may be hiding in plain sight.

Climb aboard this boat for your trip down the Amazon River.

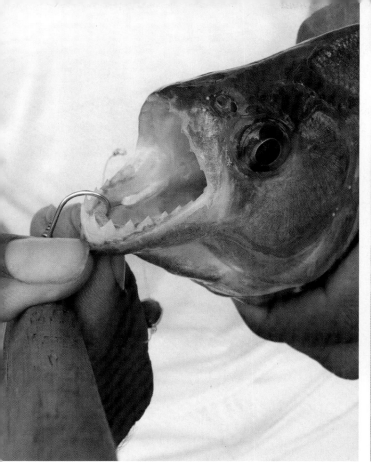

The water is muddy, but it is filled with living things. Meat-eating fish called piranhas swim in the water. They have sharp, pointed teeth to tear apart their food.

Snakes swim in the water, too. The anaconda is one of the largest snakes in the world. Do you see that wild pig along the shore? An anaconda could swallow it whole! After a big meal like that, the anaconda will not have to eat again for weeks or months!

Piranhas and anacondas live in the river.

Folks, it is time to get out of the boat and explore the land. Follow me! Stay together. Plants grow fast here. They can make it hard to find your way.

Look at that big hairy spider! It is a tarantula. It looks mean, but it will not hurt you.

And here is a poison dart frog. This one is blue, but some dart frogs are yellow, red, or green. Many have black spots. Their bright colors scare away animals that might eat them.

Tarantulas and poison dart frogs may look scary, but they do not try to hurt humans.

Listen! Do you hear that loud screech? It is a macaw parrot. It eats fruits and nuts that grow on trees. Is it squawking at us? Is it telling us to leave?

Well, folks, it is time for our amazing Amazon adventure to end. I hope you enjoyed the tour. Be sure to come back another time. You may not see the plants and animals you saw today. You may see other amazing plants and animals instead.

Macaws eat fruits and nuts that grow on trees.

What Do Plants and Animals Need to Survive?

Science Words

survive

Animals and plants are living things. What do they need to stay alive?

1. Animal Needs

Have you ever tried to hold your breath? You cannot hold it for very long because you need air.

Animals need air to **survive**. To survive means to stay alive. If animals don't get air, they die. Many animals breathe air into their lungs. Fish take in air through their gills.

NGSS **2-LS2-1.** Plan and conduct an investigation to determine if plants need sunlight and water to grow.

LS2.A. Plants depend on water and light to grow.

Cause and Effect Events have causes that generate observable patterns.

Planning and Carrying Out Investigations

Animals need water, too. Many animals get water by drinking it. The water may be in a stream or a pond. It might be drops of water on a leaf. Some animals get water from plants they eat. Some animals need a lot of water. Other animals do not need as much water.

Animals need food to survive. Animals get their food by eating plants or other animals. Mountain goats eat grass. Killer whales hunt other animals. Foxes eat berries and crickets. Some animals need a lot of food. Others do not need as much food.

This mountain goat gets food by eating grass plants.

2. Plant Needs

Animals need air, water, and food to survive. Do plants need the same things to survive?

Like animals, plants cannot survive without air. Plants get air through tiny openings in their leaves.

Plants need water, too. But plants don't drink water like animals do. Many plants take in water through their roots. The water flows up through the plant stem to the leaves.

Plants need air, water, and sunlight to survive.

This plant has wilted because it did not get enough water.

Animals eat food to survive, but plants make their own food. Green plants use air, water, and sunlight to make food in their leaves.

Plants need just the right amount of water and sunlight to stay healthy and green. If they get too much sunlight or too much water, they may not survive. If they get too little sunlight or too little water, they become weak. They may wilt and die.

Lesson Summary

Animals need air, water, and food to survive. Plants use air, water, and sunlight to make food. Without water and sunlight, plants will die.

A Honeybee Mystery

Like all animals, honeybees need air, food, and water. But are honeybees getting what they need to survive?

Honeybees live together in a group. The group is called a colony. A colony has thousands of honeybees in it. Each colony of honeybees lives in a hive.

Most of the honeybees in a colony are worker bees. They are very busy doing the work in the hive. They collect food. They keep the hive clean. They take care of baby honeybees.

Worker bees take care of this hive located in a tree.

Honeybees must eat food to survive. They collect sweet nectar from flowers. Some of the nectar they eat. Some of it they turn into honey to save for later. They store the honey in honeycombs.

How do honeybees know where to find flowers? Scouting worker bees look for them. When a worker bee finds flowers, it flies back to the hive. The worker bee does a dance. The wiggles in the dance tell the other worker bees where the flowers are.

A worker bee finds flowers and does a dance back at the hive to tell others where the flowers are.

In winter, honeybees eat the honey they stored in summer. Eating helps them stay warm. Honeybees need to keep warm to survive the winter.

They also keep warm by crowding together in a group and shivering. Shivering makes the honeybees warmer. The honeybees on the outside of the group are colder than the ones in the middle. The inside honeybees change places with the outside ones. That means no honeybee gets too cold.

Eating the honey stored in honeycombs helps honeybees stay warm in winter.

There is a honeybee mystery. They seem to be getting sick and dying. Scientists are not sure why.

Tiny animals called mites kill some honeybees. But big groups of honeybees are dying. Scientists think some plant sprays may be killing the honeybees.

Diseases are killing honeybees, too. There are many things making honeybees die. Solving this mystery might help honeybees survive.

Some plant sprays may cause honeybees to get sick and die.

How Do Plants and Animals Depend on Each Other?

Science
Words
pollen

Plants and animals do not live alone. Other living things live nearby. How do living things help each other survive?

1. Animal Survival

You know that animals need food to survive. Squirrels eat nuts. Hawks eat mice. Bears eat fish and berries. Food is one way that animals depend on the plants and other animals that live nearby.

 NGSS | **2-LS2-2.** Develop a simple model that mimics the function of an animal in dispersing seeds or pollinating plants. **LS2.A.** Plants depend on animals for pollination or to move their seeds around. | **ETS1.B.** Designs can be conveyed through sketches, drawings, or physical models. These representations are useful in communicating ideas for a problem's solutions to other people. | **Structure and Function** The shape and stability of structures of natural and designed objects are related to their function(s). |  **Developing and Using Models**

Why are the crows on the deer? They are eating ticks. Tick bites can make deer and other animals sick. The crow depends on ticks for food. The deer depends on the crow to eat the ticks.

Some animals also depend on plants for shelter. Deer sleep under trees. They stay warm and dry there. Raccoons hide in trees. Beavers cut down trees with their sharp teeth. They use the tree branches to build their homes. Turn over a plant leaf, and you may see beetles hiding there.

A tree is shelter for this raccoon.

The seeds of this burr plant can stick to an animal's fur.

2. Plant Survival

Plants help animals survive. It might surprise you to learn that animals help plants survive, too! Some plants depend on animals to move their seeds to new places.

Some plants have seeds with hooks that stick to an animal's fur. The animal carries the seed to new places. Other plants have seeds inside fruits that animals eat. The seeds pass out of the animal in its droppings. Where the seed drops, a new plant may grow.

Many plants need **pollen** from other plants to make seeds. Some depend on animals to move the pollen. When a bee gets food from a flower, pollen may stick to its legs. If the bee flies to a new flower, that plant can use the pollen to make seeds.

Plants depend on other plants, too. Some plants grow roots on trees. These plants get the water they need from the tree they grow on.

Bees help plants when they move pollen to other plants.

3. Ideas from Nature

A zipper can hold two pieces of cloth together. Buttons or snaps work, too. One engineer came up with a new idea for a fastener. He got the idea from nature.

The engineer's idea for this fastener came from nature.

The engineer was walking in the woods with his dog. He noticed that burrs stuck to his dog's fur. It was hard to get them off the dog. When he looked closely at the burrs, he saw that they had tiny hooks.

Hooks

Loops

The engineer decided to design a new kind of fastener. Engineers make drawings to share ideas. One piece would have hooks on it like the burr seeds. The other piece would have loops on it like the fur on his dog. The hooks need to hold on tight to the loops. It took many years to find the right materials.

Now people use this hook-and-loop fastener every day. It is on shoes, pants, and hats. You can even play catch with toys made with this invention.

This drawing shows how the hooks hold on to the loops.

Lesson Summary

Animals need plants for shelter and food. Plants need animals to spread their seeds around and carry pollen. Nature can give engineers ideas for ways to design new products and share ideas.

Piggyback Ride on a Crab

Some animals depend on other kinds of animals. How does a sea urchin help a crab survive?

For protection, a crab has a shell, and a sea urchin has many sharp spines.

Crabs have shells that cover their bodies. The shell protects the crab. One kind of crab has another way to protect itself. It carries a sea urchin on its back!

The sea urchin is a small, spiny animal. It moves very slowly. It lives in the ocean where the carrier crab lives. Its colorful spines move back and forth in the water. The spines are sharp! They keep enemies away.

A carrier crab crawls along the ocean floor. It looks for food. The sea urchin rides on its back. Hooks on the legs of the crab hold the sea urchin in place.

An enemy comes near! The crab buries itself in the sand. Now only the spiky sea urchin can be seen. The spikes scare away the enemy.

This piggyback ride is not for fun. The crab uses the sea urchin for protection to survive.

The sea urchin protects this carrier crab.

Why Do Plants and Animals Live in Some Places and Not in Others?

Science Words

habitat

Plants and animals live all over the world. Which places are best for different kinds of plants and animals?

1. Habitats

Plants need water and sunlight. Animals need plants or other animals for food. They need water, too.

All living things must get what they need in the place they live. If their needs are not met, the plants and animals will not survive.

NGSS **2-LS4-1.** Make observations of plants and animals to compare the diversity of life in different habitats.

LS4.D. There are many different kinds of living things in any area, and they exist in different places on land and in water.

Planning and Carrying Out Investigations

The places where plants and animals live are called their **habitats**. There are many kinds of habitats in the world. One may be cold and dry. Another may be warm and rainy.

Some plants and animals live only on land. Some live only in water. Lizards and roses live on land. Fish live in the water.

Some living things live on land and in the water. Sea turtles swim in water. But they lay eggs on land. The sea turtle's habitat includes both the land and the water.

Fish live their whole lives in water. They cannot survive on land.

2. Cold and Hot Habitats

Habitats may be cold or hot, cool or warm. A polar bear lives in a place that is cold for most of the year. Its thick fur and fat keeps it warm on the land or in the water. A polar bear would not survive in a hot place.

A camel can live in a hot habitat. It cannot survive in the same habitat as the polar bear. Camels store fat in their humps, but they have very little fat on the rest of their bodies.

Camels can live where it is very hot.

Some animals move to warmer places when their habitats get too cool. Geese fly south for the winter. They return when it gets warmer again.

Some places have a pattern of cold and hot. It may be warm during the day and cool at night. It may be hot at one time of the year and cold at another time of the year. A birch tree can only survive where it is cold in the winter and warm in the summer. It cannot survive in places that are hot or cold all year long.

A birch tree survives only in places that are cold in winter and warm in summer.

3. Wet and Dry Habitats

Some plants and animals survive best in wet habitats. These places get a lot of rain. Cattails are plants that grow in ponds. Alligators live in swamps. They could not survive in dry places.

Some plants and animals survive best in dry habitats. Cactuses are plants that survive in dry places. Camels live in dry places, too. They can go for days without water.

Habitats may be wet or dry.

4. Saltwater and Freshwater Habitats

Some plants and animals live only in salt water. Others live only in fresh water. Fresh water is not salty. Lobsters live in salt water. They cannot live in fresh water. Frogs live in fresh water. So do water lilies. They cannot live in salt water.

Most animals cannot drink salt water. They depend on fresh water to survive. Deer, beavers, and foxes drink fresh water.

Plants and animals may live in saltwater or freshwater habitats.

5. Comparing Habitats

Scientists study habitats. They measure how hot it is. They find out how much rain falls. They keep track of the days it rains. They check to see how much salt is in water. They collect all of the data.

The data help them compare habitats. One place may get more than 100 inches of rain in a year. It may rain there 250 days in a year. A dry place may get only 10 inches of rain in a year. It may rain only a few days each year.

Scientists compare how much rain falls in different habitats.

Scientists use the data they collect to find out if a habitat is getting hotter or drier.

Scientists look for patterns in data. They can use data to find out if habitats are changing. A place may be getting warmer. It may be getting drier. A water habitat may be getting saltier.

Collecting data on habitats is important work. Plants die if they get too hot. Animals die if there is not enough water to drink.

Lesson Summary

There are many kinds of habitats. Habitats may be cold or hot. They may be wet or dry. There are saltwater and freshwater habitats, too.

Disappearing Pandas

Everybody loves giant pandas. They look like big teddy bears. So, why are they disappearing?

Giant pandas eat mostly bamboo shoots and leaves. They eat bamboo 12 hours a day! Bamboo grows in thick forests in parts of China. But people are cutting down the bamboo forests to build farms and houses and roads. The giant panda's habitat is shrinking.

Now giant pandas live only in a small area in China. They live high in the mountains. The bamboo forests still grow there.

Giant pandas eat bamboo plants and not much else.

Giant pandas have few babies. A mother giant panda may have only one or two cubs every two years. What can people do to help the giant pandas survive?

Now there are places where pandas are safe. Laws protect their habitat. So, the bamboo forests cannot be cut down. Once there were few pandas left. Now there are more, but there are still very few pandas in the wild.

Giant pandas have few babies.

How Do Plants and Animals Survive in a Rainforest?

Science Words

rainforest

You learned that some living things survive best where it rains a lot. What is it like in a rainforest?

1. Rainforests

Rainforests get lots of rain. More than 70 inches of rain falls each year. Thick clouds may hang over the trees. Rainforests can seem dark. That is because they have many tall trees that grow close together. The trees block sunlight from reaching the ground.

NGSS **2-LS4-1.** Make observations of plants and animals to compare the diversity of life in different habitats.

LS4.D. There are many different kinds of living things in any area, and they exist in different places on land and in water.

Planning and Carrying Out Investigations

2. Living Things in a Rainforest

A rainforest has many trees and other plants. It is home to many kinds of animals. Birds with bright colors and loud calls may live in treetops. Monkeys with curly tails may swing from tree branches. Snakes and frogs may live in trees, too. But most of the animals in a rainforest are insects. Mosquitoes, butterflies, and ants are just a few.

Living Things in a Rainforest

Toucan

Boa constrictor

Sloth

Spider monkey

Macaw

Jaguar

Morpho butterfly

Ferns

Poison dart frog

3. Survival in a Rainforest

Rainforest plants and animals get what they need from their habitats. Plants need sunlight to survive. But it can be dark in a rainforest. Vines grow up trees so they can reach sunlight. Many plants on the forest floor have large leaves. The leaves help the plants get enough sunlight to make food.

Many plants depend on animals in the rainforest. Birds and bats eat fruits. They move the seeds to new places. Monkeys feed on tree flowers. As they lick the flowers, pollen sticks to their faces. The monkeys move the pollen to other trees.

A rainforest has many trees that grow close together.

This mother sloth is hanging on a vine.

There is plenty of food and water in a rainforest. Frogs feed on insects. Sloths eat leaves. Jaguars drink river water. Animals in the forest depend on plants for shelter and places to hide. Frogs lay their eggs on leaves. Parrots nest in trees. Sloths hang from tree branches and vines. Many animals are so well hidden that it can be hard to spot them.

Lesson Summary

Rainforests get a lot of rain. Many kinds of plants and animals live in a rainforest. They get what they need from the habitat in which they live.

A Colony of Leaf Cutters

Rainforests have animals that are big and small. How do tiny ants meet their needs?

If you visit a rainforest, you may see some ants carrying leaves above their heads. The leaves look bigger than the ants! These ants are leaf-cutter ants.

Leaf-cutter ants work together in a colony. There are many different jobs that need to be done. The queen lays eggs. These eggs grow into soldiers and workers. The soldiers protect the nest. The workers help feed the colony.

Leaf-cutter ants carry leaves above their heads.

Some workers have jaws that are strong enough to break through human skin. These workers cut out pieces of leaves. They carry them back to the nest. But the ants do not eat the leaves! Inside the nest, other workers cut the leaves into small pieces. They use these pieces to grow the food they eat.

Ants may be small, but they work together to survive. Each ant has a different job so that all the ants can meet their needs.

Workers cut out pieces of leaves with their strong jaws and carry the pieces back to their nest.

How Do Plants and Animals Survive in a Desert?

Science Words

desert

You learned that some living things survive where it is dry. What is it like in a desert?

1. Deserts

Deserts get very little rain. Less than 10 inches of rain may fall in a whole year. The sky is often clear of clouds. It can be very hot during the day, but cooler at night. Rocks, stones, and sand cover the ground.

NGSS **2-LS4-1.** Make observations of plants and animals to compare the diversity of life in different habitats.

LS4.D. There are many different kinds of living things in any area, and they exist in different places on land and in water.

Planning and Carrying Out Investigations

2. Living Things in a Desert

Only certain kinds of plants
and animals can live in a desert.
Jackrabbits, lizards, and coyotes
survive in the desert. So do some kinds
of birds and insects.

Trees and other plants grow far
apart. When it rains, plants spring to
life. Flowers bloom and make seeds.
Then the plants dry up, waiting for
the next rain.

Living Things in a Desert

Cactus

Lizard

Jackrabbit

Joshua tree

Rattlesnake

Kangaroo rat

Kit fox

3. Survival in a Desert

Deserts are very dry. But desert plants and animals have ways to get the food and water they need.

Many trees in the desert have small leaves. Plants with smaller leaves do not lose as much water. That helps plants survive where there is very little rain.

Many cactus plants have thick stems. The stems store water. A cactus can survive a long time without rain.

This cactus has thick stems where water is stored.

There is very little water to drink in a desert. Many animals get the water they need from the plants or animals they eat. Desert tortoises get water from the leaves they eat. Roadrunners get water from the lizards they catch.

A roadrunner gets water from its food.

Deserts can be hot. Some animals cool off in the shade of plants or rocks. Birds nest in holes in cactuses. Kangaroo rats dig dens under the ground. Coyotes hunt at night when it is cooler.

Lesson Summary

Deserts get very little rain. Yet many plants and animals live in deserts. They have ways to get the food and water they need to survive.

Desert Rat

It is hot. There is not much water. Enemies are close by. How does one kind of rat survive in the desert?

It is nighttime, and the desert has cooled off. A kangaroo rat comes out of its cool burrow to find something to eat. It does not have to find water. The animal gets all the water it needs from its food. The kangaroo rat does not sweat or pant either. Its body does not lose much water.

The kangaroo rat finds some seeds and mesquite beans. A pouch in its cheek holds the food. It heads back to its burrow.

The kangaroo rat comes out of its burrow at night when the desert is cooler.

The kangaroo rat has great hearing. It listens for enemies as it heads home. Owls and snakes and other animals will try to catch it. Watch out! The kangaroo rat hears an owl coming at the last second.

The kangaroo rat quickly jumps away. It has s___ back legs. It jumps and ___ a kangaroo. It can jum___ ___t feet in a single leap. Ju___ ___s it get away, so it reach___ ___ safely.

A kangaroo rat can jump over six feet.

How Do Plants and Animals Survive in a Pond?

Science Words

pond

You learned that some living things survive best in fresh water. What is it like in a freshwater pond?

1. Ponds

Ponds are small bodies of water. Most ponds contain fresh water. The water is not very deep. The temperature is al̲ the same from the top to th̲ bottom is often mu̲ ̲ay look muddy, to̲

strong
hops lik̲
over eig̲
̲mping hel̲
es its burrow

NGSS   **2-LS4-1.** Make observations of plants and animals to compare the diversity of life in different habitats.   **LS4.D.** There are ma̲ area, and they exist ̲ng and ̲g Out ̲ations

2. Living Things in a Pond

Many kinds of plants and animals live in or near a pond. In the water are pondweeds and fish. Turtles and ducks swim in the water or sit on rocks in the sun. Frogs live part of their lives in the water and part of their lives on land. Above the pond are many insects. On the land around a pond are trees and other plants. Deer and many other animals live near a pond.

Living Things in a Pond

Dragonfly

Deer

Reeds

Duck

Water lilies

Cattails

Frog

Turtle

Fish

Pondweeds

3. Survival in a Pond

Pond plants and animals get what they need from their habitat. Plants need sunlight to make their food. Pondweeds grow in shallow water where sunlight can reach the leaves. Reeds and cattails grow in the water, but their leaves are above water. Lily pads are leaves of the water lily. They float on the water.

There is plenty of food and water in a pond habitat. Frogs eat insects. Egrets feed on fish. Deer come to the pond to get water to drink. Ducks dip their heads into the water to feed on plants, fish, and insects.

A water lily has long stems that reach the bottom of the pond.

Some pond animals depend on plants for shelter and places to hide. Muskrats build shelters out of plants. Ducks make their nests among the reeds where they are hidden from view. Fish hide in pondweeds. Spiders use plants to hold their webs.

This muskrat is building a shelter with reeds.

Lesson Summary

Ponds are shallow bodies of water. Many kinds of plants and animals live in pond habitats, either in the water or on the land nearby. They get what they need from their habitat.

Water Striders

Step into water and your foot breaks through the surface. So, how can water striders walk on water?

Water striders are insects that look like giant mosquitoes. They are often called pond skaters because groups of them skate on top of a pond's surface. They look like they are ice skating. But there is no ice!

The surface of the water is like a very thin skin. When a water strider stands on the thin skin, its legs do not break through. They just make dents in the skin. The insect's weight is spread evenly among its legs.

A water strider's legs make dents in the water's surface, but they do not break through.

Water striders often skate across the water in groups.

Water striders have six legs. The front two are short. The other four are long and thin. The two middle legs act like paddles to row the insect across the water. The two back legs act like brakes. They also help the insect steer.

The body is covered with tiny hairs. The hairs shed water so it does not get wet. If it got wet, it would sink. Instead, the water strider stays on top of the water. Don't you wish you could walk on water, too?

How Do Plants and Animals Survive in the Ocean?

Science Words

ocean

You learned that some living things survive best in salt water. What is it like in the ocean?

1. The Ocean

The **ocean** is a huge body of salt water. It is shallow near the shore. It gets deeper and deeper away from the shore. Sunlight does not reach down into the ocean very far. The deepest part of the ocean is cold and dark.

 NGSS **2-LS4-1.** Make observations of plants and animals to compare the diversity of life in different habitats.

LS4.D. There are many different kinds of living things in any area, and they exist in different places on land and in water.

 Planning and Carrying Out Investigations

2. Living Things in the Ocean

Many kinds of animals live in the ocean. Most of them live near the surface. Fewer live in the deepest parts of the ocean. Fish, sea stars, crabs, eels, and squid are all animals that live in the ocean.

There are not as many ocean plants as there are land plants. Why? Plants need sunlight to make food. Sunlight cannot reach deep into the ocean.

Living Things in the Ocean

Whale

Sea turtle

Jellyfish

Crab

Fish

Shark

Sea star

Squid

3. Survival in the Ocean

Living things in the ocean get what they need from their habitat. Ocean animals need food to survive. Many animals feed on tiny living things that float in the ocean. Sea turtles eat jellyfish and sea grasses. Seals eat fish. Sea otters find shellfish and clams to eat.

Fish get the air they need through their gills. Dolphins, sea lions, and whales have lungs. They need to come to the surface to get air.

A dolphin comes to the surface for air.

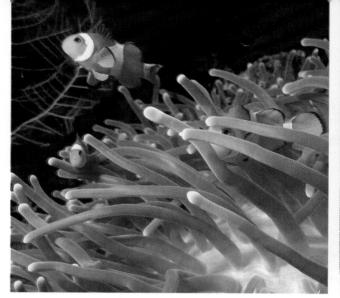

Many ocean animals need shelter and hiding places. Hermit crabs find empty shells to live in. Small fish may hide in seaweed. Some fish hide among living things that have the same color. Squid can change colors to blend in with rocks and seaweed nearby.

Some ocean animals live in groups. Killer whales live in groups called pods. Small fish often swim in large groups. A school of small fish looks like one big fish. This helps the small fish stay safe.

Ocean animals have ways to hide from danger.

Lesson Summary

The ocean is a huge body of salt water. Only certain kinds of living things can survive in the ocean. They get what they need from their habitat.

Strange Creatures of the Deep

Suppose you could go down to the deepest part of the ocean. What living things might you see?

Sunlight does not reach deep into the ocean. It is very cold and very dark. Some of the strangest creatures you have ever seen live here.

One deep-sea creature is this giant isopod. It looks like a pill bug, but it is much bigger. Giant isopods can be more than a foot long. They can live for a long time without food. They eat whatever falls down from above.

Giant isopods crawl on the sea floor.

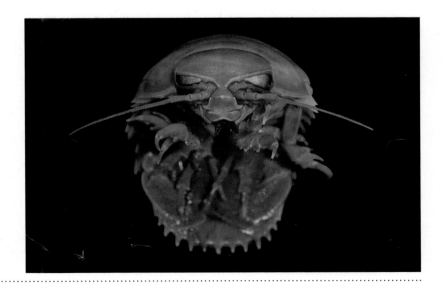

One of the strangest deep-sea creatures is the yeti crab. It is about as long as a banana. Two big claws are covered with blond, silky hairs. They make the crab look furry. Scientists think that the hairs may be used to find food in the deep sea.

The yeti crab is blind. The deep sea is so dark that the crab could not see even if its eyes worked. So, it does not need them!

The claws of the yeti crab are covered with blond, silky hairs that make it look furry.

Another strange sea creature is this sea cucumber. It looks like it is made of clear plastic. You can see its body parts inside. How would you like it if people could see inside your body?

Many arms surround a sea cucumber's mouth. The animal creeps slowly along the ocean bottom. Its arms sweep tiny pieces of food and mud into its mouth.

The body of this sea cucumber is so clear you can see its insides.

An anglerfish is strange looking, too. It has its own headlight! A rod sticks out of its head. The rod looks like a fishing pole. A light hangs at the end. The light attracts fish for the anglerfish to eat. The light also helps it see.

The mouth of an anglerfish is filled with sharp teeth. An anglerfish will eat a fish that comes too close.

These creatures may look strange. They may look scary. But they all have ways to survive in the deep sea.

An anglerfish has a mouth full of sharp teeth and its own headlight.

Materials and Their Uses

Suppose you want to build a boat. If you make a boat with paper, it would not be very strong. If you make it with glass, the boat would probably break. A concrete boat might sink. How are materials alike and different? How are they used in different ways?

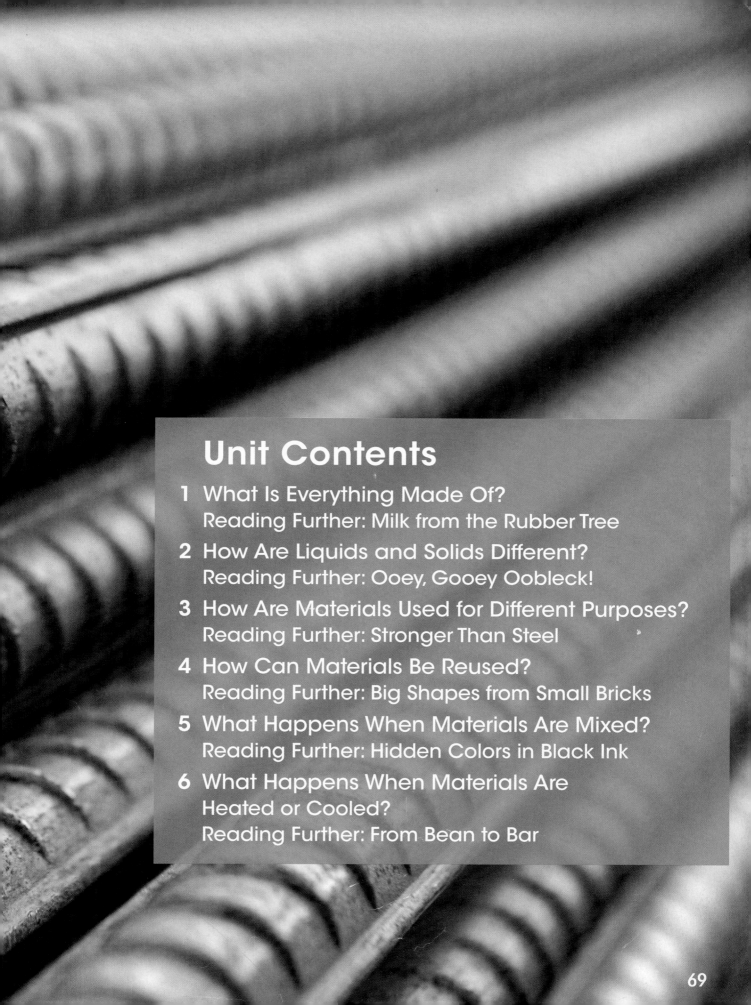

Unit Contents

Unit 2 Overview

Graphic Organizer: This unit is structured to heighten awareness of materials in the world by delving into the materials' **properties**, **uses**, and **changes**.

Properties of Materials

1. What Is Everything Made Of?

2. How Are Liquids and Solids Different?

Uses of Materials

3. How Are Materials Used for Different Purposes?

4. How Can Materials Be Reused?

Changes in Materials

5. What Happens When Materials Are Mixed?

6. What Happens When Materials Are Heated or Cooled?

NGSS Next Generation Science Standards

Performance Expectations

2-PS1-1. Plan and conduct an investigation to describe and classify different kinds of materials by their observable properties.

2-PS1-2. Analyze data obtained from testing different materials to determine which materials have the properties that are best suited for an intended purpose.

2-PS1-3. Make observations to construct an evidence-based account of how an object made of a small set of pieces can be disassembled and made into a new object.

2-PS1-4. Construct an argument with evidence that some changes caused by heating or cooling can be reversed and some cannot.

Disciplinary Core Ideas

PS1.A: Structure and Properties of Matter

- Different kinds of matter exist and many of them can be either solid or liquid, depending on temperature. Matter can be described and classified by its observable properties.

- Different properties are suited to different purposes.

- A great variety of objects can be built up from a small set of pieces.

PS1.B: Chemical Reactions

- Heating or cooling a substance may cause changes that can be observed. Sometimes these changes are reversible, and sometimes they are not.

Crosscutting Concepts

Patterns

- Patterns in the natural and human designed world can be observed.

Cause and Effect

- Events have causes that generate observable patterns.

- Simple tests can be designed to gather evidence to support or refute student ideas about causes.

Energy and Matter

- Objects may break into smaller pieces and be put together into larger pieces, or change shapes.

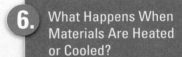 Planning and Carrying Out Investigations

Analyzing and Interpreting Data

Constructing Explanations and Designing Solutions

Engaging in Argument from Evidence

I Wonder...

What materials could I use to make a boat?

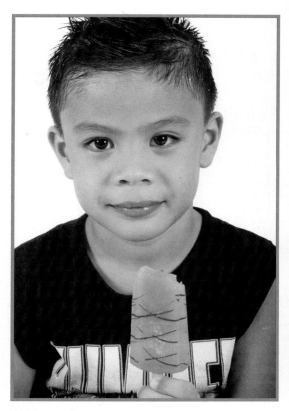

Why do some materials melt?

What materials keep me dry?

What Is Everything Made Of?

Science Words

classify

material

property

Look anywhere. You see many different things. What are the things made of?

1. Materials

You go to the park. You climb over a bridge made of wood. You go down a slide made of plastic. You play on tires made of rubber. Wood, plastic, and rubber are **materials**. A material is what an object is made of.

NGSS **2-PS1-1.** Plan and conduct an investigation to describe and classify different kinds of materials by their observable properties.

PS1.A. Different kinds of matter exist and many of them can be either solid or liquid, depending on temperature. Matter can be described and classified by its observable properties.

Patterns Patterns in the natural and human designed world can be observed.

 **Planning and Carrying Out Investigations**

A bicycle has a metal frame. It has rubber tires and a leather seat. It might have a plastic fender. It might have a mirror made of glass. The bicycle is made of many different materials.

What is your backpack made of? It might be made of cloth. It might have a metal zipper. A window might have a wood frame and glass panes. A chair might have a cloth seat and wood or metal legs. Many objects are made of more than one material.

This bicycle is made of more than one material.

A property of a rubber hose is that it bends easily.

2. Properties

Have you ever used sandpaper? Sandpaper is made of sand glued on paper. One **property** of sandpaper is that it is rough. A property is a way of describing an object.

All objects have properties. A property of a rubber hose is that it bends. A property of a glass window is that you can see through it. A property of a plastic cup is that it will not break if you drop it.

Objects have many different properties. A rock may be gray, hard, and rough. A metal pan may be hard, smooth, and shiny. A sponge is soft and bendable. You can soak up water with a sponge.

Objects made of the same material have some of the same properties. Bridges and sidewalks are made of concrete. They are strong and hard. Windows and drinking glasses are made of glass. They are breakable, and you can see through them.

This rock is gray, hard, and rough.

3. Comparing Properties

Scientists try to make sense of the world. They look closely at different objects and the materials they are made of. They **classify** objects by their properties. When they classify objects, they put them into groups so that all the things in a group have the same property.

A scientist might study objects to find out if they sink or float in water. Objects that float would go in one group. Objects that sink would go in another group.

This ring floats in water.

Do all heavy
things sink?

Next, the scientist might look for
ways the objects that float or sink are
alike. Do all heavy things sink? Why
do some objects float? Scientists ask
questions. They look for patterns.

When you sort things into groups,
you are acting like a scientist. You
study each object. You look for ways
objects are alike and different. You
decide which group each object
belongs in.

Lesson Summary

Objects are made of different materials.
They can be described and classified by their
properties. Objects made of the same materials
have some of the same properties.

Milk from the Rubber Tree

Natural rubber comes from the rubber tree. Does rubber grow on trees like apples and oranges do?

The rubber tree grows in the rainforest. Like many trees, its sap moves through its trunk. The sap looks like milk. It is often called rubber tree milk. Rubber is made with this sap.

Long ago, people discovered the special properties of this sap. It clumps up into lumpy balls. It can stretch and bend. It can be molded into different shapes. People made rubber shoes with the sap. They made bouncing balls, too.

Rubber is made from the sap of the rubber tree.

Today, rubber trees are grown on large plantations. When the trees are about six years old, workers can collect the sap. They cut a slit in the bark. The sap drips into a bowl. About six hours later, the slit dries up. The next day, they can cut a new slit in the tree.

One way to make rubber is to press and dry the sap. Now scientists can make rubber with other materials. But many things made of rubber start the same way—with rubber tree sap!

Sap from the rubber tree is collected, pressed into sheets, and dried.

How Are Liquids and Solids Different?

Science Words

liquid

solid

Objects have different properties. What properties does milk have? How is a pear different from milk?

1. Liquids and Solids

You may pour milk into a glass, or you may pour it into a bowl of cereal. Milk is a **liquid**. A liquid flows into a container. It takes the shape of the container it is poured into. Milk, juice, and water are all liquids.

 NGSS **2-PS1-1.** Plan and conduct an investigation to describe and classify different kinds of materials by their observable properties.

PS1.A. Different kinds of matter exist and many of them can be either solid or liquid, depending on temperature. Matter can be described and classified by its observable properties.

Patterns Patterns in the natural and human designed world can be observed.

 **Planning and Carrying Out Investigations**

A pear is different. It is a **solid**. A solid does not change shape when it is moved. If you put a pear in a container, it keeps its shape. A pear, a brick, and a tree are all solids.

Do you think honey is a liquid? It pours more slowly than milk. But honey is a liquid, too. If you pour honey into a jar, it takes the shape of the jar. Some liquids flow quickly, and some flow slowly.

Water is a liquid, but it can be a solid, too. If water is very cold, it turns into ice. Ice is a solid.

A pear is a solid.

Honey is a liquid.

2. Measuring Liquids and Solids

Liquids and solids have different properties. They feel different. They look different. Are they measured in different ways, too?

Orange juice is a liquid. The shape of a liquid depends on the container it is in. So, the same amount of orange juice looks different in a pitcher or in a bottle.

How much orange juice is in the pitcher or bottle? To measure a liquid, you pour it into cups. Then you count the cups.

You can measure how much orange juice is in the pitcher.

You can measure a tree with a tape measure.

Most solids cannot be measured this way. Your desk is a solid. To measure a solid, you can use a ruler. You could find out how tall, how long, and how wide the object is.

A ball is a solid. You can use a tape measure to find out how big around it is. A tape measure is a ruler that bends. What other solids can you measure?

Lesson Summary

A liquid takes the shape of the container it is poured into. A solid keeps its shape. Measuring cups are used to measure liquids. Rulers are used to measure solids.

Ooey, Gooey Oobleck!

A liquid takes the shape of its container, but a solid keeps its shape. Is there material that does both?

Have you ever heard of oobleck? It gets its name from the book *Bartholomew and the Oobleck* by Dr. Seuss. In the book, oobleck is a gooey, green material. It falls from the sky, sticks to everything, and causes all kinds of trouble.

Recipe for Oobleck

- 4 drops of green food coloring
- 1 cup of water
- 4 cups of cornstarch

Mix food coloring and water in a bowl.
Stir in cornstarch a little bit at a time.
Stop when the mix is thick.

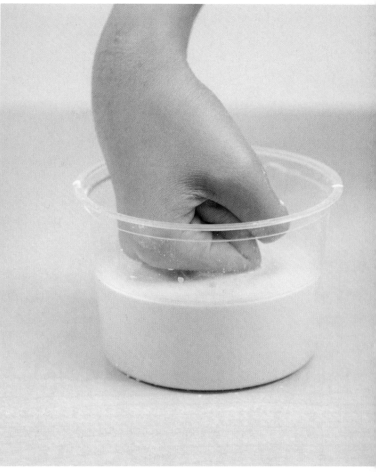

But what is oobleck? Does it act like a liquid or a solid? You can make your own oobleck to find out. Follow the directions on the recipe card. Then play with the oobleck and watch how it acts.

Move your hands slowly through the oobleck. It flows like a liquid. Now punch the surface with your fist. It holds its shape like a solid. Oobleck acts like a liquid and a solid!

Oobleck acts like both a liquid and a solid.

How Are Materials Used for Different Purposes?

Science Words

absorb

waterproof

Some materials help you stay dry in the rain. Would you use the same materials to clean up a spill?

1. Materials for Keeping out Rain

It's a warm, rainy day. You want to go outside. What will you wear?

You could wear a cotton coat. But water flows through cotton. You may get wet if you wear a cotton coat in the rain.

 NGSS **2-PS1-2.** Analyze data obtained from testing different materials to determine which materials have the properties that are best suited for an intended purpose.

PS1.A. Different properties are suited to different purposes.

Cause and Effect Simple tests can be designed to gather evidence to support or refute student ideas about causes.

 **Analyzing and Interpreting Data**

A raincoat is a better choice. Raincoats are made of material that is **waterproof**. Water does not flow through waterproof materials.

If you wear shoes in the rain, your feet might get wet. Boots made of rubber keep out the rain. One of the properties of rubber is that it is waterproof. An umbrella is also made of waterproof material.

People choose materials for a purpose. The purpose of the raincoat, the boots, and the umbrella is to keep you dry.

The purpose of an umbrella is keep you dry when it rains.

2. Materials for Cleaning Up Spills

You spill a cup of milk on the floor. Milk flows because it is a liquid. Now you need to clean up the spill. What will you use?

You could try a plastic bag. But a plastic bag does not **absorb** liquids. When objects absorb liquids, they hold on to the liquids. A plastic bag does not clean up spills very well. It does not have the property you need for this purpose.

What will you use to clean up the spill?

You could use a paper towel. Paper towels absorb liquids. Sponges absorb liquids, too. Sometimes more than one object has the right properties for a purpose.

You might think that the sponge would work best. To find out, you could perform a test. You could pour a cup of liquid on the floor in two places. You could use the paper towel to clean up one spill and the sponge to clean up the other spill. Then compare the results. Did the sponge do a better job of cleaning up the spill?

A sponge absorbs liquids.

3. Materials for Building

People use different materials to keep dry and to clean up spills. They use different materials to build things, too.

Did you ever build a tent in your home? Maybe you used a blanket and some chairs to build your tent. You chose a blanket because it is big and people can't see through it. You chose chairs because they are hard and strong and can hold up a blanket.

A blanket makes a good tent house.

A slide made of metal is hard and smooth.

Sometimes more than one property is needed for a purpose. If you want to build a slide, you choose a material that is hard and smooth so that you can go down it fast. If you go down a slide too slowly, it is not as fun.

What material would you use to make a slide? Wood might be too rough. Cardboard is smooth, but it might tear into pieces. Metal and plastic are hard and smooth, so metal or plastic might make a good slide.

4. New Ways to Use Materials

People need a way to cross a river. So, engineers design a bridge.

What properties should the bridge have? It needs to be long enough to cross the river. It needs to be strong enough to carry heavy trucks. When wind blows or rain falls, the bridge should stay standing.

Engineers make models of their designs. The model is smaller than the bridge will be. But it might be made of the materials they plan to use. The bridge might be made of wood, concrete, or steel.

A bridge needs to be strong to carry heavy trucks.

This model shows a new bridge before it is built.

Engineers test their models to see if they work. They might test the model bridge to find out how many heavy trucks could be on the bridge at one time. If the bridge bends or falls down, then the design does not work. A new design is needed.

Engineers try different designs. If a design does not work, they try another.

Lesson Summary

People use a material that is right for a purpose. Sometimes more than one kind of material has the right properties for a purpose. Engineers test designs to see what material works best for a purpose.

Stronger Than Steel

Spiders spin their webs from the silk they make. But it is not just for webs. This amazing material has other uses.

Snip off a strand of your hair. Tug on both ends. Is your hair strong? It is not as strong as spider silk. Spider silk is thinner than human hair, but it is stronger than a strand of steel. Spider silk is amazing!

Spiders make silk inside their bodies. It looks like thread when it comes out. Can you find the silk thread coming out of this spider's body?

This spider is wrapping her egg case in silk.

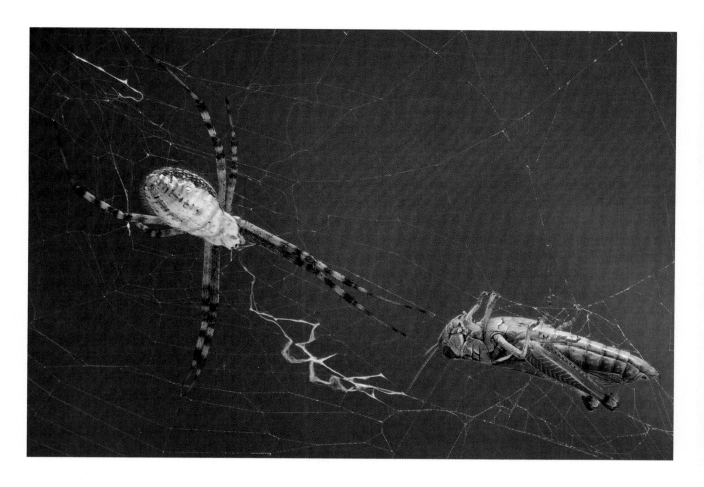

Spider silk is strong. Different types of silk have different properties. Some can stretch like a rubber band without breaking. Some can also be very sticky.

Spiders use their silk for different purposes. Some spiders wrap their egg cases in silk. Many spiders build webs to catch insects to eat. When an insect flies into a web, the silk stretches. The insect gets caught in the sticky silk. Then the spider has its meal!

A grasshopper is caught in the sticky silk of a spider's web.

Some spiders hang from the silk threads. The silk is so strong that they can jump through the air and the thread will not break.

Spider silk can help engineers design a better parachute. Parachute cords need to be strong. People need to hang on to a parachute like a spider hangs on to silk. Could spider silk be used to make parachute cords stronger?

A spider hangs by a silk thread.

There are problems with using spider silk, though. It is hard to get enough! It takes a long time to get silk out of a spider. Also, pulling silk from a spider can harm it.

So, engineers are trying to make human-made silk. They study the materials in spider silk and try to copy them. Can they make something as amazing as spider silk?

Spider silk might make parachute cords stronger.

How Can Materials Be Reused?

Science Words

reuse

You want to make a tree house or fort. Could you use materials that were once used for something else?

1. Reusing Materials

An old house is torn down. What could you do with the wood from the walls and the bricks from the chimney? You could **reuse** them. When you reuse something, you use it again in a different way.

 NGSS **2-PS1-3.** Make observations to construct an evidence-based account of how an object made of a small set of pieces can be disassembled and made into a new object.

PS1.A. A great variety of objects can be built up from a small set of pieces.

Energy and Matter Objects may break into smaller pieces and be put together into larger pieces, or change shapes.

 **Constructing Explanations and Designing Solutions**

You could use the wood boards to make a fence, a deck, or even a tree house. You could build a ladder out of pieces of wood to get up to your tree house.

The bricks from the chimney are all the same size. Many things could be made with the bricks. You could use them to make a brick walkway or wall. The shape would change, but the bricks would be the same.

Objects can be broken apart into smaller pieces. The pieces can be reused in many different ways.

Bricks from a chimney can be used to make a walkway.

2. Changing Shapes

Have you ever built a tower with blocks? How many blocks did you use?

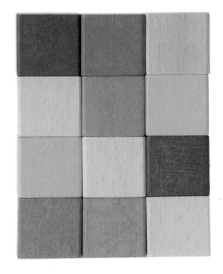

After you make a tower, you might decide to take it apart. Then you could use the pieces to make a different building. You could make a castle with the blocks. You could make a rocket ship or car. Many different buildings could be made with the same set of blocks. Each building would have a different shape.

Many different shapes can be made with one set of blocks.

This rooster is made from a ball of clay.

Clay is another material you can use to make many different shapes. One of the properties of clay is that it is easy to mold. When you mold something, you change its shape.

You could mold a ball of clay into a dinosaur or a rabbit. You could make one thing and then change it to something else. The shape changes, but the amount of clay stays the same.

Lesson Summary

Materials can be reused in many ways. Objects can be broken apart. The pieces can be used to make new objects. Some materials can be molded into new shapes.

Big Shapes from Small Bricks

This giant giraffe stands almost as tall as a building. But look closely. It is made of thousands of small pieces!

The toy bricks used to make the giraffe were invented over 50 years ago. Engineers designed the bricks to snap together. The fit is tight, but the bricks are still easy to pull apart. So, you can take apart any figure you make and use the pieces to build something new.

Many different figures can be made with the small pieces. What is the most interesting figure you have seen?

Thousands of toy bricks fit together to form this giraffe.

Up close you can see the small bricks that fit together to make these parrots.

It takes a lot of time to build a big figure like the giraffe. And, it takes a lot of planning! First, designers make drawings. They show the figure from all sides. Then they decide what bricks to use. Which shape, size, and color bricks will they use for each part?

From far away, these parrots look almost real. But up close, you can see the small pieces. Suppose you had thousands of toy bricks. What would you build?

What Happens When Materials Are Mixed?

Science Words

mixture

Suppose you mix some materials together. Do the materials change? Can they change back?

1. Mixtures

Have you ever made a fruit salad? You cut up fruit. You mix the pieces in a bowl. You can still see and taste the different pieces of fruit. Fruit salad is a **mixture** of different kinds of fruit.

 NGSS **2-PS1-1.** Plan and conduct an investigation to describe and classify different kinds of materials by their observable properties.

PS1.A. Different kinds of matter exist and many of them can be either solid, or liquid, depending on temperature. Matter can be described and classified by its observable properties.

Patterns Patterns in the natural and human designed world can be observed.

 **Planning and Carrying Out Investigations**

Chocolate milk is a mixture, too. It is a mixture of chocolate powder and milk. After you stir them together, the milk changes color. It looks and tastes different.

Do you like one kind of fruit best? You could take out that fruit from the fruit salad. But you can't take out the powder from the chocolate milk.

You can mix different things together. Sometimes you can separate the things you mixed. Sometimes you can't.

Chocolate milk is a mixture.

2. Properties of Mixtures

Mix water, flour, and salt together. What will you make?

Water is a clear liquid. Flour and salt are both white, but they taste different. If you look at flour and salt with a magnifying glass, you can see the grains. Grains of salt are bigger than grains of flour.

When you mix flour, salt, and water, you make dough. You can't get the flour, salt, or water back after you mix them.

Water, flour, and salt can be mixed together to make dough.

Look closely at the dough. Compare it to the flour, salt, and water. Dough can be molded into different shapes. It is sticky and wet. It is not dry like flour and salt. It does not flow like water. Dough has different properties from the water, salt, and flour that were used to make it.

Dough is sticky and wet.

Lesson Summary

When materials are mixed, they form a mixture. The mixture may have different properties from the materials that were used to make the mixture. After you mix materials, you may not be able to get them back.

Hidden Colors in Black Ink

What colors are in black ink? If you said black, you could be right. But you might be wrong!

Some materials are mixtures. Is black ink made with a mixture of different colors? Or is it made with just one color—black?

Here is a way to find out. With a black marker, make a dot in the middle of a piece of white filter paper. Then use a dropper to drip water on the ink mark, one drop at a time. Now watch what happens to the black ink.

You can watch the black ink separate into different colors.

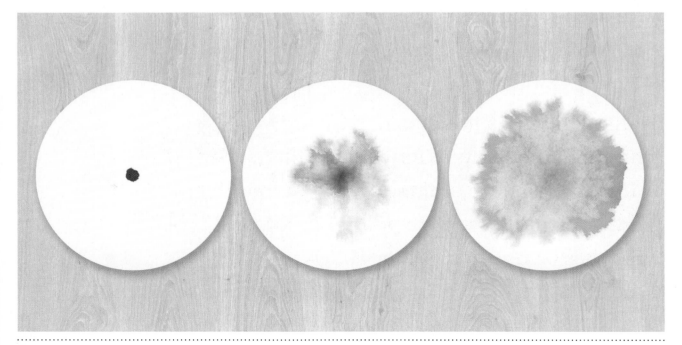

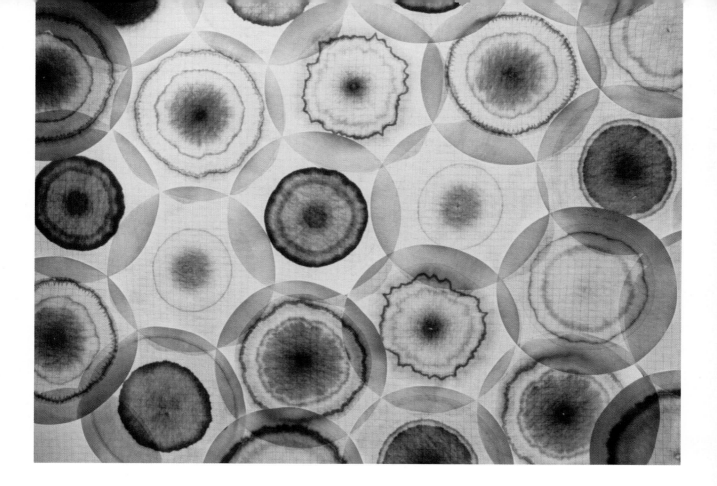

Black ink is really a mixture of colors. When water mixes with the ink, the mixture spreads out. Some colors travel farther than others. So, the colors separate.

Many inks are mixtures of different colors.

Scientists use this process to find out what materials are in colored inks. One ink may look like another. But it may be made with different materials.

Will a different kind of black marker separate into different colors? Try different markers and find out!

What Happens When Materials Are Heated or Cooled?

Science Words

freeze

melt

You can heat materials. You can freeze materials. Do the materials change when they are heated or cooled?

1. Freezing and Melting

Have you ever made an ice pop? You pour juice into a mold, and then you add a stick. You put the mold into the freezer. After the pop is in the freezer for a few hours, the liquid juice becomes solid.

NGSS **2-PS1-4.** Construct an argument with evidence that some changes caused by heating or cooling can be reversed and some cannot.

PS1.B. Heating or cooling a substance may cause changes that can be observed. Sometimes these changes are reversible, and sometimes they are not.

Cause and Effect Events have causes that generate observable patterns.

Engaging in Argument from Evidence

The ice pop is cool and refreshing on a hot summer day. But if you leave it outside, what happens? The sun heats the ice pop and causes it to **melt**. The ice pop becomes a liquid again. It started as a liquid. It became a solid. Then it changed back to a liquid again.

You can **freeze** water to make ice. You can melt ice to make water. You can change water to ice, and you can change it back again. The changes can be reversed. They can go back to the way it was before the change. Some changes can be reversed.

The sun is melting this ice pop.

2. Heating and Cooling

A cook heats water to make soup. The water starts to bubble. If the cook takes the pot away from the stove, the water cools. It stops bubbling. The change is reversed.

A cook might put solid butter in a metal pan and heat it on a stove. The butter melts. Now the cook can pour the butter because it is a liquid.

Butter changes from a solid to a liquid when it is heated.

The hot stove melted the butter but not the metal pan. Some materials need higher temperatures to melt.

Factories heat metal until it is very hot. The metal changes from gray to orange. Hot metal is easier to bend. It can be shaped into pans or car parts. When the metal cools, the color changes back to gray. The metal becomes hard again.

When water, butter, or metal is heated or cooled, its properties change. Can you think of other materials that change when they are heated or cooled?

Metal changes when it is heated.

Popcorn cannot change back to corn seeds.

3. Changes That Cannot Be Reversed

When metal is heated, it melts. When it is cooled, it goes back to being hard again. The changes to the metal are reversed.

Have you ever popped corn to eat? Popcorn begins as small, hard, yellow seeds. When you heat the seeds, they change. They pop into big, white, crunchy puffs. Popped corn cannot change back to corn. You cannot make it small, yellow, and hard again. The changes to popcorn cannot be reversed.

Pizza dough is soft and wet. Heating the dough in a hot oven causes the dough to change into pizza crust. Pizza crust is firm and dry. You cannot change pizza crust back to soft dough.

When wood burns, it heats the air and glows. Then it changes to a gray powder called ashes. Ashes cannot change back to wood. Even when the ashes cool, they are still a gray powder.

Ashes cannot change back to wood.

4. Clues to Causes

Two scientists are exploring a forest. They see signs of changes. Ashes cover the ground beneath a tree. The bark on the tree is black. A metal trash can has melted. A pinecone has burst open. The changes are clues for the scientists.

The scientists suspect that there was a fire in the forest. They know that when wood burns, it leaves ashes on the ground. Fire can make bark black. Metal melts only if it gets very hot. Some pinecones open up only when there is a forest fire.

This burned tree is a clue that there was a fire in the forest.

Scientists are like detectives. They look closely at things. They look for patterns and clues. They try to figure out the causes for the things they see.

Do you like being a detective? You might want to be a scientist, too.

These burned cans are clues that there was a fire in the forest.

Lesson Summary

When materials are heated or cooled, they may change their properties. Sometimes the changes can be reversed. Sometimes the changes cannot be reversed. Scientists look for the causes of the changes they see.

From Bean to Bar

Do you like beans? Not everyone does. But did you know that chocolate is made from beans?

Chocolate is made from the beans of the cacao tree. Cacao beans grow inside large pods about the size of a football. The white beans are covered in a wet, sticky material. The beans are bitter. It takes many steps to make sweet chocolate from cacao beans. Each step changes the properties of the beans.

The pods are the fruit of the cacao tree.

First, the pods are opened and covered for a few days. The pods break down. The beans turn brown and are less bitter.

Next, the beans are spread out in the sun. They are turned often so they do not stick. The sun dries the beans. It is important that they dry evenly. Now there is less water inside the beans, so they weigh less.

The cacao beans dry in the sun.

Then the beans are cleaned and roasted in ovens. The hot oven changes the properties of the beans. The beans turn darker. A rich cacao flavor is formed. The shells become brittle. Machines remove the shells. The heart of the bean that is left is called a *nib*.

Next, heavy wheels grind the nibs. Once again the properties change. The moving wheels heat the nibs. The nibs melt into a smooth, thick chocolate paste.

These cacao nibs are used to make chocolate.

Chocolate bars are made with cacao beans.

The chocolate paste is separated into cocoa butter and cocoa powder. The properties of these products are different from the chocolate paste. Cocoa butter is a clear, golden liquid. Cocoa powder is dry, brown powder. These and other materials are mixed to make different kinds of chocolate.

Take a bite of a chocolate bar. The warmth of your mouth melts it. You change its properties one last time. Yum!

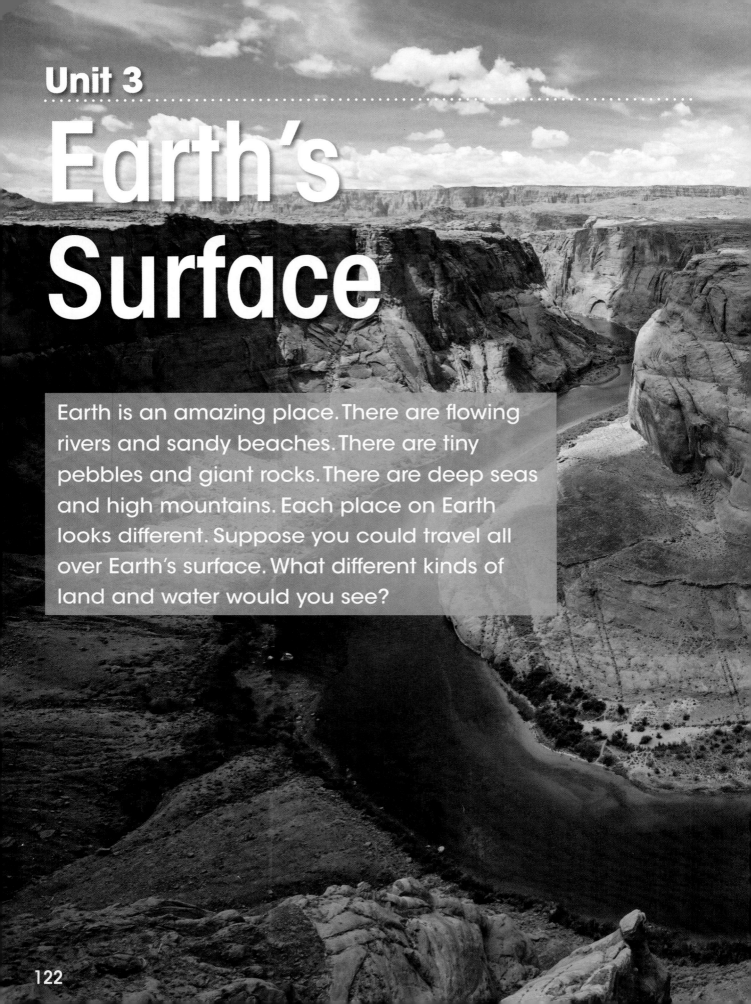

Unit 3

Earth's Surface

Earth is an amazing place. There are flowing rivers and sandy beaches. There are tiny pebbles and giant rocks. There are deep seas and high mountains. Each place on Earth looks different. Suppose you could travel all over Earth's surface. What different kinds of land and water would you see?

Unit Contents

Unit 3 Overview

Graphic Organizer: This unit is structured to explore **Earth's surface**, including how it can be **described** and how it **changes** over time.

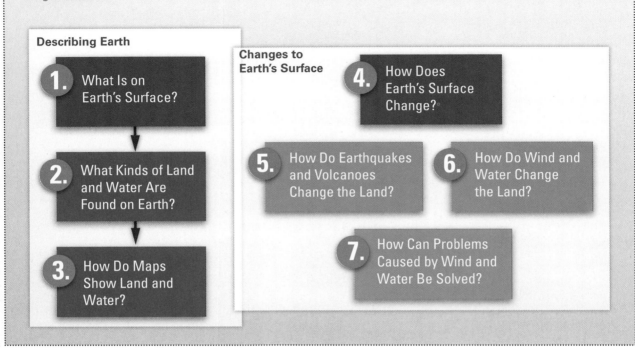

Describing Earth

1. What Is on Earth's Surface?

2. What Kinds of Land and Water Are Found on Earth?

3. How Do Maps Show Land and Water?

Changes to Earth's Surface

4. How Does Earth's Surface Change?

5. How Do Earthquakes and Volcanoes Change the Land?

6. How Do Wind and Water Change the Land?

7. How Can Problems Caused by Wind and Water Be Solved?

NGSS Next Generation Science Standards

Performance Expectations

2-ESS1-1. Use information from several sources to provide evidence that Earth events can occur quickly or slowly.

2-ESS2-1. Compare multiple solutions designed to slow or prevent wind or water from changing the shape of the land.

2-ESS2-2. Develop a model to represent the shapes and kinds of land and bodies of water in an area.

2-ESS2-3. Obtain information to identify where water is found on Earth and that it can be solid or liquid.

Disciplinary Core Ideas

ESS1.C: The History of Planet Earth

• Some events happen very quickly; others occur very slowly, over a time period much longer than one can observe.

ESS2.A: Earth Materials and Systems

• Wind and water can change the shape of the land.

ESS2.B: Plate Tectonics and Large-Scale System Interactions

• Maps show where things are located. One can map the shapes and kinds of land and water in any area.

ESS2.C: The Roles of Water in Earth's Surface Processes

• Water is found in the ocean, rivers, lakes, and ponds. Water exists as solid ice and in liquid form.

ETS1.C: Optimizing the Design Solution

• Because there is always more than one possible solution to a problem, it is useful to compare and test designs.

Crosscutting Concepts

Patterns

• Patterns in the natural world can be observed.

Stability and Change

• Things may change slowly or rapidly.

 Developing and Using Models

 Obtaining, Evaluating, and Communicating Information

 Constructing Explanations and Designing Solutions

I Wonder...

What is on Earth's surface?

How do waves change the land?

What do different places on Earth look like?

What Is on Earth's Surface?

**Science
Words
globe
soil**

Suppose you are an astronaut looking down on Earth from space. What would you see?

1. Earth from Space

From space, a lot of Earth's surface looks blue. That's because most of Earth's surface is covered by water. Land areas look green or brown from space. White areas may be clouds. But they may also be places covered with ice or snow.

NGSS **2-ESS2-3.** Obtain information to identify where water is found on Earth and that it can be solid or liquid.

ESS2.C. Water is found in the ocean, rivers, lakes, and ponds. Water exists as solid ice and in liquid form.

Patterns Patterns in the natural world can be observed.

Obtaining, Evaluating, and Communicating Information

You don't need to be an astronaut to look at Earth's surface. You can look at a **globe**. A globe is a model of Earth. It is shaped like Earth. On a globe, you can see the land and water areas on Earth's surface.

Look at the land and water on the globe. Think about traveling on land. It is not possible to go all the way around Earth just on land. Now think about traveling on water. You can go all around Earth on water.

A globe is a model of Earth.

2. Earth's Land

When you are outdoors, look closely at the land beneath your feet. What materials do you see on the ground?

Some of Earth's surface is covered with rocks. Rocks may be large enough to climb or so small you can hold several in your hand. You can feel them beneath your feet in a stream. You may see rocks sticking out of rivers or oceans. Rocks are many colors and shapes. Some rocks are very hard, and others are softer. Some are rough, and some are smooth.

Rocks are found on Earth's surface.

Some of Earth's surface is covered with sand. Sand is made up of small bits of rock. You can find sand on beaches near lakes and oceans. Sand is also found in deserts.

Some of Earth's surface is covered with **soil**. Soil is the top, loose layer of Earth's surface in which plants grow and some animals live. Soil may be dark and wet. Without soil, many plants would not be able to survive.

Sand and soil are found on Earth's surface.

3. Earth's Water

You can find water in many places on Earth's surface. Most of Earth's water is found in the ocean. Water is also found in rivers and lakes.

Some water on Earth's surface is salt water. Some is fresh water. Salt water is salty. Fresh water is not salty. Oceans have salt water. Most rivers and lakes have fresh water. Some rivers and lakes are salty. Some are a mix of fresh and salt water.

Ocean water is salty.

Water on Earth can be liquid or solid. In some places on Earth, thick layers of ice stay frozen solid all year long. In other places, water freezes when it is cold and melts when it is warm. Water in lakes and rivers can be liquid in the summer and solid in the winter.

Some lakes freeze when it is cold.

Lesson Summary

Some of Earth's surface is land. Most of it is water. Land areas are covered with rocks, sand, or soil. Water on Earth's surface may be salty or fresh. It can be liquid or solid.

Puzzling Planet

Look at the land areas on a globe. They are big pieces of Earth's puzzle!

Find Africa and South America. Do they look like they could fit together like pieces of a giant puzzle?

The shapes of the land areas gave some scientists an idea. Maybe the land areas were not always separated by ocean. Maybe at one time, they were connected. It seemed like a crazy idea to many people.

Africa and South America look like they could fit together like pieces of a puzzle.

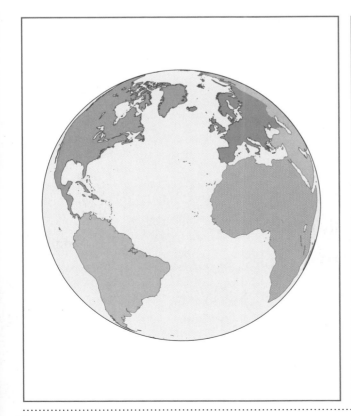

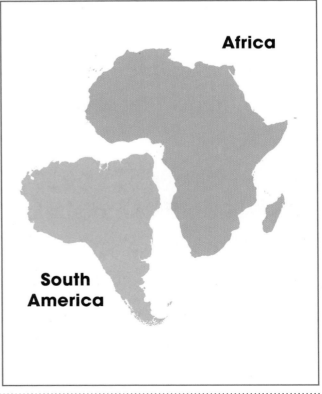

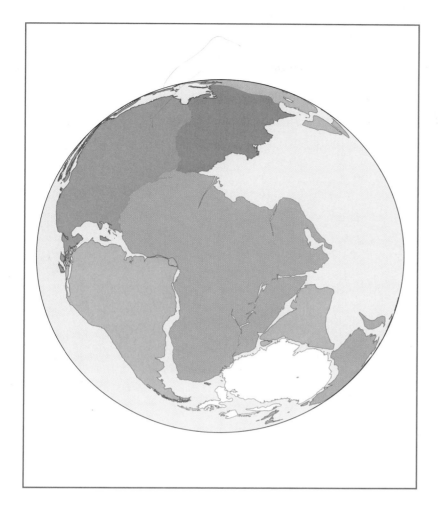

Scientists found evidence that Earth's land areas were once connected.

Scientists wanted to know if the idea was true or not. So, they measured the coastlines. They looked for evidence in the rocks and living things. They studied dinosaur bones. Scientists looked on both sides of the ocean.

Today, most scientists believe that all land areas on Earth were connected. This idea came from looking at the shapes of the land areas. But without evidence, it was just an idea.

What Kinds of Land and Water Are Found on Earth?

Science Words

glacier

island

lake

river

valley

Earth's surface has many kinds of land and water. Which ones can you name?

1. Mountains and Valleys

Mountains are the highest kind of land on Earth. Mountains can be steep and rocky. Some have pointed tops. Hills are high, but not as high as mountains. **Valleys** are low places that lie between mountains or hills. They can be narrow or wide.

 NGSS **2-ESS2-3.** Obtain information to identify where water is found on Earth and that it can be solid or liquid.

ESS2.C. Water is found in the ocean, rivers, lakes, and ponds. Water exists as solid ice and in liquid form.

Patterns Patterns in the natural world can be observed.

 **Obtaining, Evaluating, and Communicating Information**

2. Rivers and Streams

Most valleys have **rivers** moving through them. A river is water that flows across land. Small rivers are called streams. Rivers and streams flow downhill into a larger river, lake, or ocean.

What would happen if you put a toy boat in a river? Water in rivers may move quickly or slowly. But the water is always moving. The water would carry away your toy boat.

Rivers flow downhill.

The ocean covers much of Earth's surface.

3. The Ocean

If you look out at the ocean from the shore, it may seem like it goes on forever. The ocean is very big.

The ocean is the salty water that covers much of Earth's surface. The water in the ocean is always moving, but it doesn't move like a river does. The water in the ocean flows in many directions. The water in the ocean has big waves, too. You may have seen waves crashing on the shore.

4. Lakes and Ponds

Lakes are bodies of water with land all around them. Most lakes have fresh water, but some are salty. Wind can cause lake water to move in waves, but the waves are not as big as ocean waves.

Ponds are small lakes. They are not as deep as lakes. Pond water may move a bit from wind, but water in ponds does not move very much.

Lakes have land all around them.

5. Glaciers

Glaciers are areas of thick ice that stay frozen all year long. They form when snow is packed down into ice. The frozen water that forms a glacier is fresh water, not salty. Glaciers may have small stones or large rocks in them.

Some glaciers cover large areas of flat land. Others form in high mountain areas. Glaciers move very slowly. Parts of glaciers can break off and fall into the ocean.

Glaciers stay frozen all year long.

6. Islands

Islands are areas of land with water all around them. There are islands in lakes, rivers, ponds, and the ocean. Have you ever been on an island?

Some islands are small, flat, and sandy. Other islands are much larger. They may have mountains and valleys. They may have lakes and rivers. Not all islands are round. Some are long and narrow.

Islands have water all around them.

Lesson Summary

Many kinds of land and water are found on Earth's surface. Land areas may be mountains, hills, valleys, or islands. Water is found in the ocean, lakes, ponds, rivers, streams, and glaciers.

A Long River Journey

Salmon leave the ocean for just one reason—to lay eggs. But the long journey is not easy.

Many fish live in either salt or fresh water. Salmon live in both. Adult salmon live most of their lives in the ocean. But they lay their eggs in fresh water. They return to the river or stream where they were hatched to lay their eggs.

This journey may be hundreds or thousands of miles long. It may take them to high mountains. Suppose you could follow a salmon's journey. What would you see?

Salmon leave the ocean to lay their eggs in freshwater rivers or streams.

The journey starts where a river enters the ocean. The land on either side of the river may be steep and rocky or level and sandy. Most rivers are wide near the ocean, but they get narrower and narrower.

River water is not salty like ocean water. It flows differently, too. The water moves in one direction—to the ocean. Salmon must swim in the other direction—up the river. So, moving water pushes against the salmon.

Salmon swim upriver against the flow of the water.

Many smaller rivers and streams flow into the bigger river. Salmon swim up the smaller rivers or streams to the place where they will lay their eggs. Rocks may block their way. But rocks are not a problem for salmon. Salmon can leap over rocks.

Rocks and waterfalls may not stop a salmon. But human-made dams will. Dams are too tall for salmon to leap over.

Salmon can leap over waterfalls as they swim up the river.

To help salmon get around the dams, people build fish ladders. Salmon jump the ladders just like they leap over natural rocks.

The journey ends where the salmon lay their eggs. Baby salmon hatch from the eggs. After many months, the young salmon make their own long river journey. They swim the other direction, all the way to the ocean. But this time the trip will be a little easier. They will be swimming downriver.

People build fish ladders so that salmon can swim around dams.

How Do Maps Show Land and Water?

Science Words

compass

compass rose

map key

Has your family ever used a map on a trip? How did the map help you?

1. What Maps Show

You can look at a map to see what kinds of land and water are in an area. You can see the shapes of the land and water areas. You can compare the sizes of land and water areas, too. You can use a map to find out how to go from one place to another.

NGSS **2-ESS2-2.** Develop a model to represent the shapes and kinds of land and bodies of water in an area.

ESS2.B. Maps show where things are located. One can map the shapes and kinds of land and water in any area.

Patterns Patterns in the natural world can be observed.

Developing and Using Models

Look at the Trout Lake Trail Map. Can you find any islands on the map? Which island is larger? What trail would you take to get to Mud Pond? You can learn a lot about the land and water in an area from a map.

How could you make a map of the land and water where you live? You might start by looking at a picture of the area from above. Then you would draw the land and water so that it is the same shape and in the same place as it is in the picture. Now you can use your map to help you find your way from one place to another.

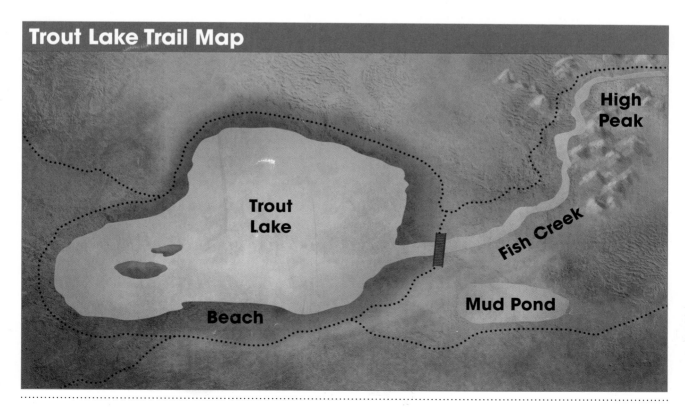

Trout Lake Trail Map

High Peak

Trout Lake

Fish Creek

Beach

Mud Pond

2. Reading Maps

What can you learn from this map of Oregon? What do the symbols mean?

Many maps use symbols to show different kinds of land and water. A **map key** explains what the symbols mean. You can use the key to find mountains, rivers, and lakes on the map of Oregon.

You can look for patterns. Most of the mountains are in one area. Many of the rivers flow into the ocean. You can often find patterns on a map.

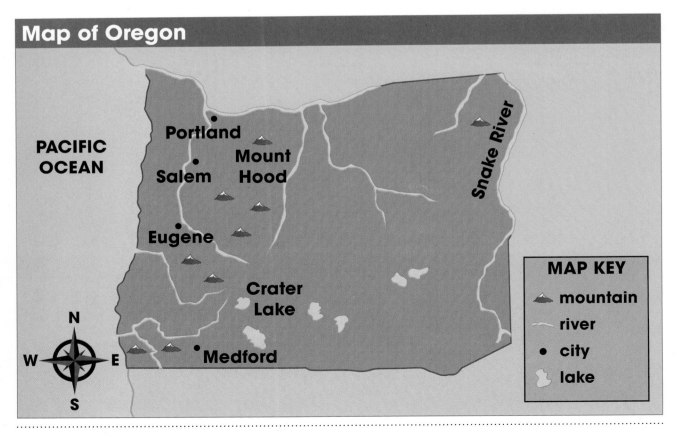

Map of Oregon

PACIFIC OCEAN

Portland

Salem

Mount Hood

Eugene

Crater Lake

Medford

Snake River

N
W   E
S

MAP KEY
- mountain
- river
- city
- lake

You can use a compass to find out what direction you are going.

A **compass** is a tool that shows direction. North, south, east, and west are directions. A **compass rose** looks like a compass. It shows directions on a map. What do you think N, S, W, and E stand for?

Look at the compass rose on the map of Oregon. Mount Hood is north of Crater Lake. People living in Medford would go east to get to the Snake River. They would go west to get to the ocean.

Lesson Summary

You can learn about the land and water in an area by looking at a map. A map key explains what the symbols on a map mean. A compass rose shows directions on a map.

Racing with a Map

Get your map and compass. On your mark, get set, go! What kind of race is this?

Orienteering is an outdoor sport. An orienteer uses a map and a compass to get from place to place on the map.

Suppose you are an orienteer. Your task is to finish a course. Each course is made up of places to visit called control sites. You can spot a control site by its white and orange marker. On the map, control sites are numbered. You must go to the sites in order. You punch a card at each site to prove you were there.

An orienteer uses a map and a compass to find each site.

What is the best route to take to each site? You decide! You may go over a hill or cross a stream because it is faster. You may go around a fallen tree or a boulder because it is easier.

Orienteering can be a race. You win by finishing the course with the fastest time. Orienteering can also be just a hike. Go with your family or try it with a friend. The idea is to be outdoors and to have fun!

A family decides the best way to get to a control site.

How Does Earth's Surface Change?

Science Words

flood

landslide

Think about a hill or a pond near you. Do you think it will look the same 100 years from now?

1. Earth's Changes

Maybe you visited a place that you haven't seen in a long time. Does it look different? Has it changed since you last saw it? Earth's surface is always changing. Land you see today may have looked different before.

 NGSS **2-ESS1-1.** Use information from several sources to provide evidence that Earth events can occur quickly or slowly.

ESS1.C. Some events happen very quickly; others occur very slowly, over a time period much longer than one can observe.

Stability and Change Things may change slowly or rapidly.

 **Constructing Explanations and Designing Solutions**

You can see some changes when they happen. A rock may slide down the side of a hill. Heavy rain may make big puddles in a yard.

Some changes take place little by little, so they are harder to notice. A pond may not be as deep as it once was. The water may not be as clear. Rocks that were under water may now be sticking above water.

If you go back to the place again when you are older, will it look the same? Any place you visit may change a little, or it may change a lot.

This pond was deeper ten years ago.

2. Fast and Slow Changes

Changes to Earth's surface can happen very fast. A **flood** can change the land in just a few hours. In a flood, water covers land that was dry before. Plants that grew on the dry land are suddenly under water.

A **landslide** can change the land in a few minutes. In a landslide, soil and rocks move from higher ground to lower ground. The land changes fast in a landslide.

A landslide changes the land quickly.

Some changes to Earth's surface happen slowly. They take a long time. Much of Earth's land was once covered with glaciers. The glaciers melted very slowly. We now see hills and lakes where the glaciers were.

Changes to Earth's surface can take a few seconds, a few days, a few years, or thousands of years.

A glacier covered this area 15,000 years ago. The glacier slowly changed the land.

Lesson Summary

Earth's surface changes. Some changes happen quickly. Other changes happen slowly over a long time.

The Trail to Exit Glacier

On a trip to Alaska, a family visits a glacier. How is the glacier changing? Here is the story the family tells.

It is a summer day. We are on a family trip to Alaska. We have seen grizzly bears and moose. Our photo album will be full of amazing pictures. Now we are hiking to a glacier.

We can see Exit Glacier in the distance. It looks like a patch of white snow. Snow falls in winter where we live, but it melts before summer comes. A glacier is different. It stays frozen all year long.

We follow the trail to the edge of Exit Glacier.

Along the trail, we come to a sign, then another, and another. One says 1926. Another says 1978. "What do the signs mean?" we ask a ranger.

The ranger explains that the glacier is changing. "In 1978, when I was a child, the edge of the glacier was where this sign is. Today, we have to walk much farther to get to the glacier. The land you are walking on was underneath the glacier just 40 years ago!"

In 1978, the edge of the glacier was where the sign is.

When Exit Glacier melts, a river of water flows downhill.

"Why is the glacier getting smaller?" we wonder. The ranger tells us that each winter, snow falls on the glacier. The new snow packs down the old layers of snow to form ice. In the warm summer months, some of the ice melts.

"Look," the ranger says. He points to the water pouring down from the glacier. "If more ice melts in summer than is added in winter, the glacier gets smaller."

Finally, we reach the edge of the glacier. A huge wall of blue and white ice towers above us. We see deep cracks in the wall. We hear cracking noises and chunks of ice falling to the ground. It is cold near the glacier.

We wonder where the edge of the glacier will be when we are grown up. How will the glacier change? Will all the ice be melted where we are standing now? We decide to come back and see for ourselves.

The cold, blue glacier towers above us.

How Do Earthquakes and Volcanoes Change the Land?

Science Words

earthquake

lava

seismograph

volcano

The ground shakes. A volcano erupts. How do these events change Earth's surface?

1. Earthquakes

Earthquakes make the ground shake. They happen when rocks change position below Earth's surface. The movement may be near Earth's surface. It may also be far below the surface.

 NGSS | **2-ESS1-1.** Use information from several sources to provide evidence that Earth events can occur quickly or slowly. | **ESS1.C.** Some events happen very quickly; others occur very slowly, over a time period much longer than one can observe. | **Stability and Change** Things may change slowly or rapidly. |  Constructing Explanations and Designing Solutions

People feel the ground shaking from some earthquakes. But many earthquakes are not very strong. People do not feel them. Small earthquakes happen every day.

The shaking usually lasts a few seconds. But earthquakes can change Earth's surface. The land can change very fast. Earthquakes can cause Earth's surface to crack open. Pieces of rock and land may be pushed up from the ground. Buildings, bridges, and trees may fall down. Some earthquakes cause large ocean waves. These large waves can flood dry land.

The land can change fast in an earthquake.

Lava flows from a volcano.

2. Volcanoes

A **volcano** is an opening in Earth's surface. The opening is often at the top of a cone-shaped mountain. A volcano may be quiet for many years. But if it erupts, it changes Earth's surface. Rock and ash may be thrown high into the air. Melted rock called **lava** may flow from the opening. When lava cools, it turns into hard rock.

The land changes fast when a volcano erupts. The shape of a mountain may change. One side may be blown off. A tall mountain can become even taller. Part of the mountain may break off. Volcanoes that erupt under the ocean can form new islands.

Rock and ash from the volcano may cover the land for miles around. Places where trees grew may now be covered with hard rock.

This island was formed by a volcano erupting.

3. Studying Earth

When will a volcano erupt? No one knows for sure. But scientists want to know. So, they study Earth. They try to find out what causes a volcano to erupt. They look for patterns.

Scientists have learned about one pattern. A lot of small earthquakes in an area may mean that a volcano is about to erupt there. The earthquakes may be so small that people cannot feel them.

There may have been many small earthquakes nearby before this volcano erupted.

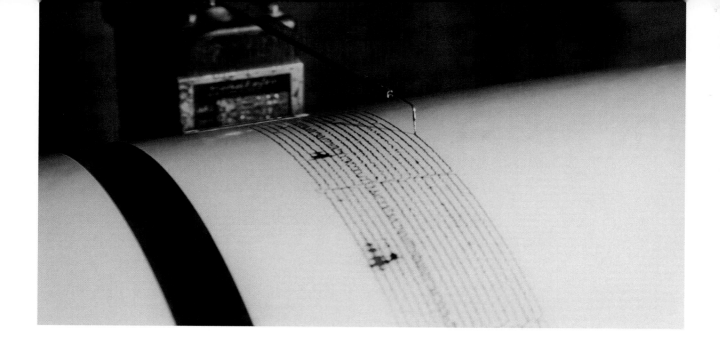

Scientists use a tool called a **seismograph** to measure earthquakes. A needle on this tool goes back and forth all of the time. It makes lines on paper. When there is an earthquake, the lines are longer.

Suppose a seismograph near a volcano records many earthquakes. Scientists can warn people who live in the area. Then the people can move to a safe place.

A seismograph measures earthquakes.

Lesson Summary

Earthquakes and volcanoes change Earth's surface. These changes happen fast. Scientists try to predict when a volcano will erupt.

The Missing Mountain Top

If you look at Mount St. Helens, it looks like its top is missing. How did the mountain lose its top?

Mount St. Helens was once the fifth highest peak in Washington state. It was shaped like a cone. Each year, people visited Mount St. Helens to camp and hike. They swam and boated in nearby Spirit Lake.

But Mount St. Helens is a volcano. For years, the volcano was quiet. Then in 1980, many small earthquakes shook the earth. Scientists knew that the volcano was now active.

Mount St. Helens was shaped like a cone.

On May 18, part of Mount St. Helens slid away in a huge landslide. Seconds later, the volcano erupted. Clouds of steam, ash, and rocks blasted high in the air. The giant clouds hid the sun. Day seemed like night.

In moments, the shape of the volcano changed. Parts of the mountain crumbled. A crater formed where the top of the mountain used to be.

Ash, steam, and rocks blasted out of Mount St. Helens in 1980.

Parts of the forest were destroyed by the eruption.

The area around the volcano changed quickly. The once forested land was nothing but gray ash. The blast knocked down trees. Landslides carried trees, mud, and rocks down the mountain and into Spirit Lake. The heat of the blast melted ice and caused floods.

The eruption lasted for nine hours. Many living things died or lost their homes. The mountain was now bare.

What is Mount St. Helens like now? The volcano is still active. Small eruptions have happened since 1980. Lava flows inside the crater have hardened into a small hill. The volcano is rebuilding.

Over time, new plants have grown. Animals that once lived there have returned. Each year, thousands of climbers hike up to the crater rim to visit the mountain's missing top.

New plants have started to grow around Mount St. Helens.

How Do Wind and Water Change the Land?

Science Words

cliff

sandbar

sand dune

Earthquakes and volcanoes change the land. Can wind and water change the land, too?

1. Wind and Water

Did you ever walk in a sandy place on a windy day? Did you feel grains of sand hitting your face? Wind can pick up sand and carry it through the air. Wind can be strong.

NGSS **2-ESS1-1.** Use information from several sources to provide evidence that Earth events can occur quickly or slowly.

ESS1.C. Some events happen very quickly; others occur very slowly, over a time period much longer than one can observe.
ESS2.A. Wind and water can change the shape of the land.

Stability and Change Things may change slowly or rapidly.

Constructing Explanations and Designing Solutions

Water can be strong, too. If you point a hose at the ground, the water may be strong enough to make a hole. The water pushes the soil away.

Water in waterfalls is strong enough to push rocks away. Rainwater is also strong. So is water in a river or stream.

Wind and water can move sand, rocks, and soil to new places. Earthquakes and volcanoes change the land quickly. Wind and water can change the land quickly, too, but many changes from wind and water happen very slowly over a long time.

Water can move rocks, sand, and soil.

2. Sand Dunes

A **sand dune** is a hill of sand made by the wind. Sand dunes can be found in deserts and on beaches near oceans or lakes.

Little by little, the wind changes the size and shape of a sand dune. The wind blows sand off the sand dune. It blows sand onto the sand dune. A tall sand dune may become shorter or longer. A sand dune with a round top may become flat. As long as the wind keeps blowing, the sand keeps moving.

Wind can change the shape of the sand dunes.

3. Rainfall

When it rains, some water soaks into the ground. But not all of it soaks in. Some water flows over the land.

Rainwater moves quickly down steep hillsides. Little streams form where the water flows. The streams cut a path in the land. The water picks up soil from the hillside. It carries the soil downhill. When the rain stops, the land has changed.

Rainwater flowing down a hillside can change the land.

Fast-moving water picks up rocks, sand, and soil.

4. Rivers

Water in a fast-moving river rushes over rocks. It splashes and swirls.

The water in a river can move very fast. As it moves, it picks up sand from the bottom of the river. It carves away rocks and soil from the land at the edge of the river. The water carries the sand, rocks, and soil along.

In some parts of a river, the water slows down. The rocks, sand, and soil carried by the water drop to the bottom of the river. Rocks may pile up. Sandy places called **sandbars** may form in the river.

Water changes the shape and size of the land under a river. The river bed may become deeper or wider. Water changes the land on the edge of a river, too. Little by little, the shore may be cut away by the river. These changes happen slowly over a very long time.

Slow-moving water drops rocks, sand, and soil.

5. Ocean Waves

Ocean waves beat against land all the time. Waves can carry sand, rocks, and seashells onto beaches. New beach areas can form. Some waves can wash away the sand, making the beach smaller.

Ocean waves pick up and carry sand and rocks.

Waves cause rocks in the water to rub against each another. The rocks wear down and get smoother. They break down into smaller and smaller pieces. The very small pieces are sand.

Ocean waves wear away the land.

Big ocean waves can cut away at rock along the shore. Over time, **cliffs** form. Cliffs are high, steep rock walls. Waves pounding on the cliffs can also carve out caves in the rock wall.

Ocean water is always moving. It causes many changes to the land. Some of these changes happen quickly. Rocks and sand may suddenly fall from a cliff. But most of the changes take place over a long time. The changes are so small you may not even notice them.

Lesson Summary

Wind and water change the land. They can pick up rocks, sand, and soil and put them in new places.

Statues Carved by Nature

People carve stone statues. Can nature carve statues out of rock, too?

These strange-looking statues in the photographs were not carved by people. They were formed by water and ice. People call them hoodoos.

Hoodoos can be found all over the world. Some hoodoos are no taller than you are. Some are taller than a ten-story building. A hoodoo you see today took hundreds of years to form. In another hundred years, the hoodoo will look much different.

These hoodoos were formed by water and ice.

How do hoodoos get their special shape? Some of the rock is harder than other parts of the rock. It is easier for rain and ice to carve the softer rock than the harder rock. If the harder rock is at the top, the hoodoo looks like a mushroom or a person wearing a hat.

People enjoy naming hoodoos. One is called Thor's Hammer. Another is called Queen's Head. What names would you give these hoodoos?

The rock that formed Thor's Hammer and Queen's Head is hardest at the top.

How Can Problems Caused by Wind and Water Be Solved?

Science Words

levee

windbreak

Wind and water change the land. What problems do these changes cause? How can the problems be solved?

1. Problems Caused by Wind and Water

A family builds a new home near a river. Rain falls for many days. The river floods the land where the family plans to live. The floodwater gets into the house and damages the new carpets and floors. Too much water can cause problems for people.

 NGSS **2-ESS2-1.** Compare multiple solutions designed to slow or prevent wind or water from changing the shape of the land.

ESS2.A. Wind and water can change the shape of the land.
ETS1.C. Because there is always more than one possible solution to a problem, it is useful to compare and test designs.

Stability and Change Things may change slowly or rapidly.

 **Constructing Explanations and Designing Solutions**

Sometimes wind can cause problems, too. A farmer plants corn seeds in a field. The soil is rich. There is plenty of sun and rain.

In a few months, the farmer expects the field to be filled with tall corn plants. But the plants do not grow. Each day wind blows across the field. The wind picks up the rich soil and carries it away. Without the rich soil, the corn plants cannot survive.

If the wind blows the soil away, these corn plants will not survive.

This windbreak protects the farmland from the wind.

2. Protection from Wind

A strong wind can blow sand or snow onto roads or highways. It can blow away soil on farms. What can be done to protect land from the wind?

One way to block the wind is called a **windbreak**. A windbreak is a row of trees or shrubs. The trees or shrubs slow down the wind. Windbreaks are used on beaches to keep wind from carrying away the sand. They can also be used to keep snow from drifting onto highways. Farmers create windbreaks to keep soil and seeds from blowing away.

Planting grasses or other small plants in windy areas can also protect the land. That's because plant roots hold sand and soil in place. The wind does not blow away as much sand or soil when plants are growing in an area.

When it is windy, plant roots help hold soil in place.

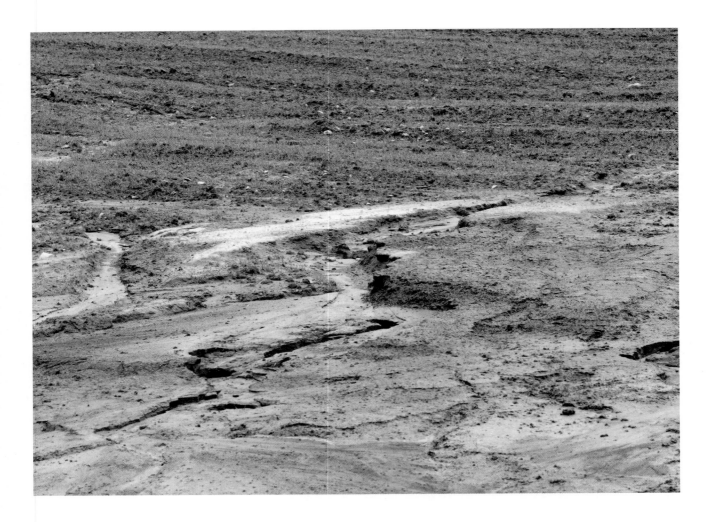

Rainwater can wash away soil.

3. Protection from Water

In a heavy rainfall, the ground cannot soak up all the water. So, some water flows over the land, washing soil away. If plants are growing in the ground, their roots hold the soil in place. Plant leaves are useful, too. They keep the water from reaching the soil all at one time. Plants growing in the area keep both the rain and wind from carrying away too much soil.

Floods can cause damage to homes and buildings. One way to protect them is by building a **levee**. A levee is a wall of soil, stones, or concrete that keeps water from flooding dry land. Many levees are built along rivers.

Levees solve problems. They can create problems, too. River water carries sand and soil. When rivers flood, they bring the rich soil to farmland. With a levee, this rich soil does not reach farmland.

This levee protects land from floods.

4. Solving Problems Caused by Wind or Water

There is a problem. A road was built near some sand dunes. The wind blows sand onto the road. When people drive on the road, it can be hard to see.

Engineers think of ways to solve problems like this. One idea may be to build a wall between the road and the sand dunes. Another idea may be to plant a windbreak of trees along the road. Growing plants on the sand dunes is another idea. Grasses planted on sand dunes may hold the sand dunes in place. Sometimes there are many ways to solve a problem.

Wind blows sand onto the road.

Which idea is best? To find out, engineers test their ideas to see how well they work. They compare the designs in many ways. A wall may cost more than the other ideas. A windbreak or wall may block the view of the sand dunes. Comparing and testing different ideas help people find the best way to solve a problem.

Grasses help hold the sand dunes in place.

Lesson Summary

Too much wind and water can cause problems for people. Windbreaks and levees are two ways to protect the land from wind and water. Engineers design and test ways to protect the land.

A Special Day for Trees

One million trees is a lot of trees. Why did people plant that many trees in just one day?

J. Sterling Morton looked out on his farm in Nebraska. The land was flat and treeless. Gusty winds blew the soil away. Morton remembered living in New York as a boy. There were so many trees there.

Morton had an idea. He knew that planting trees helps keep the soil in place, so he planted trees as windbreaks. The trees would protect his soil from the wind. Nearby, farmers planted windbreaks, too.

The farmland in Nebraska was flat and had few trees.

But Morton wanted more trees. As a newspaper reporter, he wrote about why trees are important. Trees are good windbreaks. They can be used for fuel and building materials. Trees can also provide shade from the hot sun.

People all over Nebraska listened. On April 10, 1872, they planted more than one million trees in one day! The day was called Arbor Day. *Arbor* means tree. Today all 50 states celebrate Arbor Day by planting trees.

People celebrate Arbor Day by planting trees.

Science and Engineering Resources

Have you ever looked closely at a flower? Or built things out of blocks? Then you have practiced science and engineering! You will learn how to practice these things safely.

But what is science? Science helps people learn about the world. Scientists ask questions. They gather evidence. They use evidence to answer their questions. Scientists make new discoveries. So, answers to science questions can change.

What do engineers do? They find ways to solve problems. They use science. Engineers might build a new machine. Or they might think of a new way to do something.

Science Safety

Science investigations are fun. Use these rules to keep safe before, during, and after an investigation.

Classroom Science Safety

✓ Wear safety goggles when needed.

✓ Wear safety gloves when needed.

✓ Wear an apron if needed.

✓ Tie back long hair.

✓ Tie back loose clothing.

✓ Have only investigation materials on tables.

✓ Carry equipment safely.

✓ Handle living things with care.

✓ Do not place anything in your mouth during investigations.

✓ Do not eat or drink during investigations.

✓ Tell your teacher right away if something spills or breaks.

✓ Tell your teacher right away if someone gets injured.

✓ Place waste where your teacher tells you to.

✓ Wipe down your work area.

✓ Wash your hands after cleaning up.

✓ Know your school's safety rules and follow them.

Outdoor Science Safety

✓ Wear clothes to protect you from ticks and insects.

✓ Wear a hat.

✓ Wear shoes that cover the whole foot.

✓ Wear sunscreen.

✓ Go indoors if weather is harsh.

✓ Do not touch plants or animals without permission.

✓ Never taste anything you find outdoors.

✓ Wash your hands with soap and water when you are done.

✓ Make sure an adult brings a first-aid kit.

Planning Investigations

✓ Choose safe materials.

✓ Plan how you will handle the materials safely.

✓ Do not carry out your investigation without permission.

How Can You Be a Scientist or Engineer?

Asking Questions and Defining Problems

You can be a scientist. You can ask questions about the world around you. You can act like an engineer. You can find problems to solve.

You can ask, "How can I stay warm?"

Developing and Using Models

You can use models to show real things. A model is like the real thing in some ways. But it is not exactly like the real thing.

You can make a model to show how to pollinate flowers.

Planning and Carrying Out Investigations

You can answer science questions by investigating. You can test designs to solve engineering problems. You will need to choose materials. Next plan what you will do. Then you will observe or measure.

You can investigate how shadows form.

Analyzing and Interpreting Data

You can record your findings. They are called data. You might draw, write, or use a computer. Next you look for patterns. Then you can compare what you learned to your predictions.

You can compare bridges to find the best building materials.

Using Mathematics and Computational Thinking

You can use math to answer many science questions. Counting and numbers can also help solve real-world problems.

Constructing Explanations and Designing Solutions

When you do science, you explain how things work. You talk about the evidence you found. When you solve problems, you show your design.

You can design structures to keep cool.

Engaging in Argument from Evidence

You will make claims with your evidence. You can compare your ideas with each other. You will use evidence to support your ideas and claims.

Obtaining, Evaluating, and Communicating Information

You can get science and engineering information in different ways. You can read books. You can search online. You can share what you learn with others.

You can find out how animal parents take care of their young.

Using Science and Math Skills

How Do You Make a Bar Graph?

Sometimes in science you collect data in categories. You might have found what kinds of pets your classmates have. They have dogs, cats, and fish. You record how many students have each kind of pet. You can make a table to do this.

A table is one way to look at your data. This table shows how many pets students in a class have.

Pet	How many
Dog	|||||||
Cat	||||||||||
fish	|||||||||

There were six dogs and eight cats. There were seven fish.

Now you make a bar graph. It shows how many classmates had each kind of pet. The dog column is six high. The cat column is eight high. The fish column is seven high.

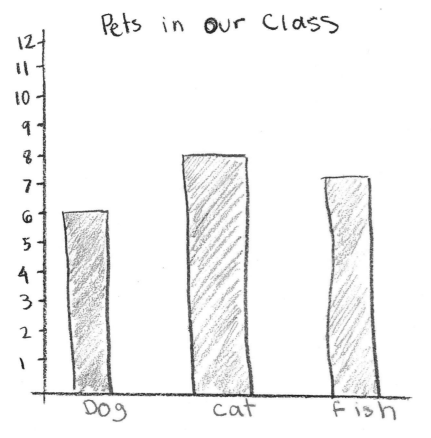

You can then make a bar graph with your data, like this one.

How Long Is It?

You can use a measuring tape or a ruler to measure lengths. Measuring tapes and rulers have marks that show length.

Each mark is the same distance from the mark before it. The marks are usually one centimeter or one inch apart.

You can use a measuring tape to measure length. It has marks to show an object's length.

To use a ruler, find the 0 cm mark. Line it up with one end of the length you are measuring. Hold the ruler along the length.

Find the mark nearest to the other end of the length. Look at the number. This is the measurement.

This drawer is about 20 cm long.

How Much Is There?

How can you tell someone how much juice you have? You can measure it!

First, find many small cups. Each cup should be the same size.

Carefully pour the juice into the cups. Don't spill any! How many cups does the juice fill up?

How much juice is in this pitcher? You can pour it into small cups to find out.

If you have a lot of juice, you can use bigger cups. If you only have a little juice, you should use smaller cups.

You can measure other things with cups. You can measure water, sand, or salt. What other things can you measure with cups?

There were 4 cups of juice in the pitcher.

absorb

A sponge absorbs water.

classify

You can classify objects into things that float or things that sink.

cliff

A cliff is a high, steep rock wall.

compass

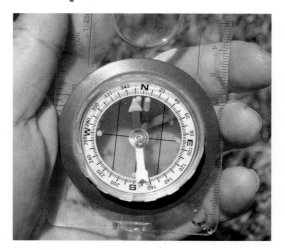

A compass is a tool that shows direction.

compass rose

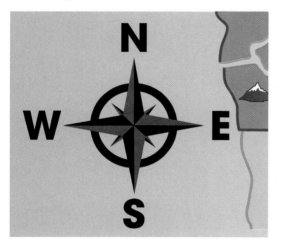

A compass rose shows direction on a map.

desert

A desert is a place that gets very little rain.

earthquake

An earthquake makes the ground shake.

flood

In a flood, water covers land that was dry before.

freeze

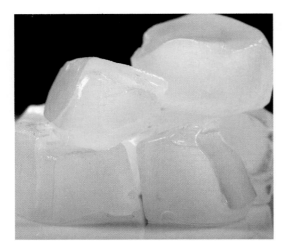

When water gets very cold, it freezes.

glacier

A glacier is an area of thick ice that stays frozen all year.

globe

A globe is a model of Earth.

habitat

A habitat is a place where a plant or animal lives.

island

An island is land with water all around it.

lake

A lake is a body of water with land all around it

landslide

In a landslide, rocks and soil move from higher land to lower land.

lava

Lava is melted rock that flows from a volcano.

levee

A levee is a wall that keeps water away from dry land.

liquid

A liquid flows. It has the shape of its container.

living thing

Plants and animals are living things.

map key

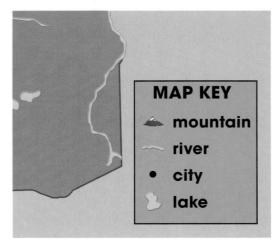

A map key tells what the symbols on a map mean.

material

Objects are made of materials. A tire is made of rubber.

melt

When an ice pop gets warm, it melts.

mixture

This fruit salad is a mixture of different fruits.

ocean

The ocean is the large body of salt water that covers much of the Earth.

pollen

Plants use pollen to make seeds.

pond

A pond is a small lake.

property

A property of this rock is that it is hard.

rainforest

A rainforest is a place that gets a lot of rain.

reuse

When wood is reused, it is used again.

river

A river is water that flows across land.

sandbar

A sandbar is a sandy place in a river.

sand dune

A sand dune is a hill of sand made by the wind.

seismograph

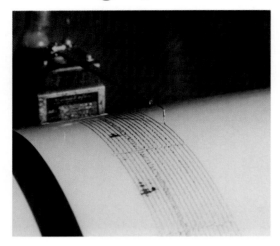

A seismograph is a tool that measures earthquakes.

soil

Soil is the top layer of land where plants grow.

solid

A solid keeps its shape when it is moved.

survive

To survive means to stay alive.

valley

A valley is a low area between mountains or hills.

volcano

A volcano is an opening in Earth's surface.

waterproof

The raincoat is waterproof. It keeps you dry.

windbreak

A windbreak is a row of trees or shrubs used to block the wind.

CREDITS

Cover and Title Page
iStockphoto

Front Matter
iii: Hxdbzxy/Dreamstime
viii: FocusTechnology/Alamy
ix: Cultura Creative/Alamy
x: Monty Rakusen/cultura/Corbis
xvi: Olaf Speier/Shutterstock
xviii: Hxdbzxy/Dreamstime
xx: Fotofeeling/Westend61/Corbis

Unit 1, Unit Opener
xxii-1: Olaf Speier/Shutterstock
3 TR: Juriah Mosin/Dreamstime
3 TL: Photowitch/Dreamstime
3 B: Darren Green/Shutterstock

Unit 1, Lesson 1
4: Thinkstock **5:** Nordjordet/
Dreamstime **6 TL, TR, C, CR,
BL, BC, BR:** Nikolai Sorokin/
Dreamstime **6 TC, CL:** Dmitry
Ersler/Dreamstime **7:** Tracy
King/Dreamstime **8 TL, CL,
BR:** atm2003/Shutterstock **8 TC,
BL:** Alex Alekseev/Shutterstock
8 BC, CR: ImagesEurope/
Alamy **9:** Thinkstock
10: Stefano Lunardi/Dreamstime
11 L: Bruce Macqueen/Dreamstime
11 R: Gedewe/Dreamstime
12: iStockphoto **13 L:** Alentejano /
Dreamstime **13 R:** Shutterstock
14 L: Thinkstock **14 R:** iStockphoto
15: KAMONRAT/Shuttestock

Unit 1, Lesson 2
16: StockPhotoAstur/Dreamstime
17: Thinkstock **18:** Thinkstock
19: Evan66/Dreamstime
20: Dssimages/Dreamstime
21 L: Michael Avory/Dreamstime
21 R: Shutterstock **22:** Dainis
Derics/Dreamstime **23:** Thinkstock

Unit 1, Lesson 3
24: Claire Tomlinson/Alamy
25: Steve Byland/Dreamstime
26: Dagobert1620/Dreamstime
27: Ned Yeung/Dreamstime
28: Aurinko/Dreamstime
28: Stocksnapper/Dreamstime
30 L: Gilles Mermet/Science Source
30R: Rodferris/Dreamstime **31:** Hal
Beral VWPics/SuperStock

Unit 1, Lesson 4
32: Yvonne Pijnenburg-
Schonewille/Shutterstock
33: Mikhail Malyshev/Dreamstime
34: Paul Cowan/Dreamstime
35 L: Ilene MacDonald/Alamy
35 R: Ilene MacDonald/Alamy
36 L: Christopher Meder/
Dreamstime **36 R:** jkirsh/
Shutterstock **37 L:** Ethan Daniels/
Shutterstock **37 R:** Thinkstock
38: Meryll/Dreamstime
39: Orangeline/Dreamstime
40: Riverrail/Dreamstime
41: Ocean/Corbis

Unit 1, Lesson 5
42: Fabrizio Cianella/Dreamstime
44 B: Antonio Jorge Nunes/
Shutterstock **44 T:** Vera Kailova/
Dreamstime **45:** Brian Magnier/
Dreamstime **46:** Kim Taylor/
Nature Picture Library/Corbis
47: Alex Wild/Visuals Unlimited/
Corbis

Unit 1, Lesson 6
48: Kcmatt/Dreamstime **50:** Raja
Rc/Dreamstime **51:** Digital Blue/
Shutterstock **52:** Thinkstock
53 B: Photographerlondon/
Dreamstime **53 T:** Michael
Durham/Minden Pictures/Corbis

Unit 1, Lesson 7
54: Jakezc/Dreamstime **56:** Ethan
Daniels/Shutterstock **57:** Vibe
Images/Alamy **58:** Shutterstock
59: Exactostock/SuperStock

Unit 1, Lesson 8
60: Krzysztof Odziomek/
Dreamstime **62:** Sokolov Alexey/
Shutterstock **63 L:** David Mckee/
Dreamstime **63 R:** Wouter
Roesems/Dreamstime **64:** Sonke
Johnsen/Visuals Unlimited/Corbis
65: ASSOCIATED PRESS **66:** Larry
Madin/WHOI/Corbis **67:** Doug
Perrine/Alamy

Unit 2, Unit Opener
68-69: Hxdbzxy/Dreamstime
71 TL: Westend61/SuperStock
71 B: Blend Images/SuperStock
71 TR: Kitsen/Dreamstime

Unit 2, Lesson 1
72: Sanchai Khudpin/Shutterstock
73: IMAGEMORE Co., Ltd./Alamy
74: Erikstefanowski/Dreamstime
75: Loris Eichenberger **76:** Diego
Vito Cervo/Dreamstime **77:** Zagor/
Dreamstime **78 L:** Likephotoman/
Dreamstime **78 R:** Eknarin
Maphichai/Dreamstime
79 T: Chan Yew Leong/Dreamstime
79 B: Trainman32/Dreamstime

Unit 2, Lesson 2
80: Ocean/Corbis **81 L:** Bara22/
Shutterstock **81 R:** Ljupco
Smokovski/Dreamstime **82:** Oleksii
Lukin/Dreamstime **83:** Ocean/
Corbis

Unit 2, Lesson 3
86: Beau Lark/Corbis
87: Ambrozinio/Dreamstime
88: Alptraum/Dreamstime **89:** Jenn
Huls/Shutterstock **90:** Randy
Faris/Corbis **91:** Thinkstock
92: Skylightpictures/Dreamstime
93: vasilkovaya/iStockphoto
94: Fotosearch **95:** Cathy Keifer/
Dreamstime **96:** Melany Sarafis/
Getty Images **97:** Digital Vision/
Getty Images

Unit 2, Lesson 4
98: Cultura Creative/Alamy
99 L: Mgd/Dreamstime
99 R: Castrothecigar/Dreamstime
100: Jiri Hera/Dreamstime
100: Jiri Hera/Dreamstime
101: Corbis **102 R:** Rayisa Nalivayko/
Dreamstime **102 L:** Shutterstock
103: Camille Tsang/Dreamstime

Unit 2, Lesson 5
104: Draftmode/Dreamstime
105: Blend Images/Alamy
106: Alexander Traksel/
Dreamstime **107:** Eric Audras/
Onoky/Corbis **109:** Geoff
Tompkinson/Science Source

Unit 2, Lesson 6
110: Picstudio/Dreamstime
111: Brent Hofacker/Shutterstock
112: Joy Brown/Shutterstock
113: Andrey N Bannov/
Shutterstock **114 L:** JIANG
HONGYAN/Shutterstock
114 R: Alexandra Lande/
Shutterstock **115 T:** Mares Lucian/
Shutterstock **115 B:** Melissa
E Dockstader/Shutterstock
116: Jaypetersen/Dreamstime
117: Cirilopoeta/iStockphoto
118 R: Saiko3p/Dreamstime
118 L: Shutterstock
119: Joshua Rainey/Dreamstime
120: Marek Uliasz/Dreamstime
121: Shutterstock

Unit 3, Unit Opener
122-123: Fotofeeling/Westend61/
Corbis **125 B:** Shutterstock
125 TR: Darrinhenry/Dreamstime
125 TL: Thinkstock

Unit 3, Lesson 1
126: NASA/Corbis **127:** Monkey
Business Images/Dreamstime
128 B: Pavel Losevsky/
Dreamstime **128 T:** Kaspri /
Shutterstock **129 L:** Simon Greig/
Dreamstime **129 R:** Brad Calkins/
Dreamstime **130:** Tom Dowd/
Dreamstime **131:** Phil MacD
Photography/Shutterstock
133 B: ArchieMkDesign /
Shutterstock

Unit 3, Lesson 2
134: Manuela Klopsch/Dreamstime
135 B: Elultimodeseo/Dreamstime
135 T: Jy604/Dreamstime
136: Elena Elisseeva/Dreamstime
137 B: Liz Van Steenburgh/
Shutterstock **137 T:** Marinko
Bradasic/Dreamstime **138:** Jf123/
Dreamstime **139:** Thinkstock
140 L: Marco Jimenez/
Dreamstime **140 R:** iStockphoto
141 T: Welcomia/Dreamstime
141 B: Modfos/Dreamstime
142: Thinkstock **143 T:** iStockphoto
143 B: Shutterstock

Unit 3, Lesson 3
144: Juice Images/Alamy
147: Robert Matton AB/Alamy
148 L: Thinkstock **148 R:** Pavla
Zakova/Dreamstime **149:** Peter
Cade / Getty Image

Unit 3, Lesson 4
150: BanksPhotos/iStockphoto
151: Kushnirov Avraham/
Dreamstime **152:** Apisit
Sriputtirut/Alamy **153:** Ralf
Broskvar/Dreamstime **154:** Accent
Alaska.com/Alamy **155:** Rich Reid
/ Getty Images **156:** Albertoloyo/
Dreamstime **157:** Rich Reid / Getty
Images

Unit 3, Lesson 5
158: John Nakata/Corbis
159: Sdubi/Shutterstock
160: Patrick Barry/Dreamstime
161: luigi nifosi/Shutterstock
162: moodboard/Alamy **163:** Ted
Foxx/Alamy **164:** USGS/Alamy
165: Everett Collection Inc/Alamy
166: Everett Collection Inc/Alamy
167: Thinkstock

Unit 3, Lesson 6
168: Vladimir Ivanov/Dreamstime
169: David Morton/Dreamstime
170: Kurt Cotoaga/Dreamstime
171: Global Warming Images/
Alamy **172:** Tom Grundy/Alamy
173: Patrick Lin/Shutterstock
174: Laurentiu Iordache/
Dreamstime **175:** idiz/Shutterstock
176: Mkojot/Dreamstime
177 L: Michael Madsen/
Dreamstime **177 R:** Christopher
Rawlins/Dreamstime

Unit 3, Lesson 7
178: blueflames/iStockphoto
179: Juice Images/Alamy
180: Fotosearch **181:** Brandon
Blinkenberg/Dreamstime
182 T: Wayne HUTCHINSON/
Alamy **182 B:** Janis Ozols/
Dreamstime **183:** Terry Smith
Images Arkansas Picture Library/
Alamy **184:** Alex Fairweather/
Alamy **185:** Dima_Rogozhin/
Shutterstock **186:** Benkrut/
Dreamstime **187 T:** Littleny/
Dreamstime **187 B:** moodboard/
Alamy

Back Matter
189: David Young-Wolff/
Alamy **190:** Thomas Barwick/
Getty Images **191:** xefstock/
Getty Images **192:** Hero Images/
Getty Images **193:** Blend Images/
Ariel Skelley/Getty Images
204: Shutterstock **205:** Thinkstock
208 TL: Jenn Huls/Shutterstock
208 TR: Diego Vito Cervo/
Dreamstime**208BL:**idiz/Shutterstock
208 BR: Robert Magorien/
Dreamstime **209 BL:** Sdubi/
Shutterstock **209 BR:** BanksPhotos/
iStockphoto **210 TL:** Picstudio/
Dreamstime **210 TR:** Jf123/
Dreamstime **210 BL:** Monkey
Business Images/Dreamstime
210 BR: Yvonne Pijnenburg-
Schonewille/Shutterstock
211 TL: Thinkstock **211 TR:** Liz
Van Steenburgh/Shutterstock
211 BL: Apisit Sriputtirut/
Alamy **211 BR:** Patrick Barry/
Dreamstime **212 TL:** Terry
Smith Images Arkansas Picture

Library/Alamy **212 TR:** Ljupco
Smokovski/Dreamstime
212 BL: Nordjordet/Dreamstime
213TL: SanchaiKhudpin/Shutterstock
213 TR: Brent Hofacker/Shutterstock
213 BL: Draftmode/Dreamstime
213 TL: Ned Yeung/Dreamstime
214 BL: Loris Eichenberger
215 TL: Cultura Creative/
Alamy **215 TR:** Elultimodeseo/
Dreamstime **215 BL:** Patrick Lin/
Shutterstock **215 BR:** Kurt Cotoaga/
Dreamstime **216 TL:** Ted Foxx/
Alamy **216 TR:** Brad Calkins/
Dreamstime **216 BL:** Bara22/
Shutterstock **216 BR:** Thinkstock
217 TL: Manuela Klopsch/
Dreamstime **217 TR:** moodboard/
Alamy **217 BL:** Beau Lark/Corbis
217 BR: Fotosearch